T0305930

On the Road to Resilience

This book delves into the critical realm of trust management within the Internet of Vehicles (IOV) networks, exploring its multifaceted implications on safety and security which forms part of the intelligent transportation system domain.

IoV emerges as a powerful convergence, seamlessly amalgamating the Internet of Things (IoT) and the intelligent transportation systems (ITS). This is crucial not only for safety-critical applications but is also an indispensable resource for non-safety applications and efficient traffic flows. While this paradigm holds numerous advantages, the existence of malicious entities and the potential spread of harmful information within the network not only impairs its performance but also presents a danger to both passengers and pedestrians. Exploring the complexities arising from dynamicity and malicious actors, this book focuses primarily on modern trust management models designed to pinpoint and eradicate threats. This includes tackling the challenges regarding the quantification of trust attributes, corresponding weights of these attributes, and misbehavior detection threshold definition within the dynamic and distributed IoV environment.

This will serve as an essential guide for industry professionals and researchers working in the areas of automotive systems and transportation networks. Additionally, it will also be useful as a supplementary text for students enrolled in courses covering cybersecurity, communication networks, and human factors in transportation.

Sarah Ali Siddiqui is a CSIRO Early Research Career (CERC) Fellow in the Cyber Security Automation and Orchestration Team, Data61, Commonwealth Scientific and Industrial Research Organisation (CSIRO), Australia.

Adnan Mahmood is a Lecturer in Computing – IoT and Networking at the School of Computing, Macquarie University, Sydney, Australia.

Quan Z. (Michael) Sheng is a Distinguished Professor and Head of the School of Computing, at Macquarie University, Sydney, Australia.

Hajime Suzuki is a Principal Research Scientist at the Cybersecurity & Quantum Systems Group, Software and Computational Systems Research Program, Data61, Commonwealth Scientific and Industrial Research Organisation (CSIRO), Australia.

Wei Ni is a Principal Scientist at the Commonwealth Scientific and Industrial Research Organisation, a Technical Expert at Standards Australia, a Conjoint Professor at the University of New South Wales, an Adjunct Professor at the University of Technology Sydney, and an Honorary Professor at Macquarie University, Sydney, Australia.

On the Road to Resilience

Ensuring Secure IoV Networks

Sarah Ali Siddiqui, Adnan Mahmood,
Quan Z. Sheng, Hajime Suzuki
and Wei Ni

CRC Press
Taylor & Francis Group
Boca Raton London New York

CRC Press is an imprint of the
Taylor & Francis Group, an **informa** business
A CHAPMAN & HALL BOOK

Designed Cover Image: High angle aerial bird's eye drone view of a country road near Sydney, New South Wales, Australia, leading through a partly burnt forest affected by the devastating bushfire season end of 2019. Stock photo

First edition published [2025]
by CRC Press
2385 NW Executive Center Drive, Suite 320, Boca Raton FL 33431

and by CRC Press
4 Park Square, Milton Park, Abingdon, Oxon, OX14 4RN

CRC Press is an imprint of Taylor & Francis Group, LLC

ISBN: 978-1-032-72352-5 (hbk)
ISBN: 978-1-0327-2350-1 (pbk)
ISBN: 978-1-032-72366-2 (ebk)

DOI:10.1201/9781032723662

Typeset in Nimbus Roman
by KnowledgeWorks Global Ltd.

Publisher's note: This book has been prepared from camera-ready copy provided by the authors.

To my beloved husband, since the moment you entered in my life, you have been the unwavering support, the cherished companion, and the love that fills each page in every chapter of this journey with warmth. This book stands as a testament to the inspiration you bring into my world. I dedicate this book to you with heartfelt gratitude for being my constant source of strength and encouragement.

Sarah Ali Siddiqui

To my loving wife, Fatima, and beloved children, Rafay, Talha, and Anna, for their love and support.

Adnan Mahmood

To my mum for her unconditional and everlasting love. To my wife, Stella, and my daughters, Fiona and Phoebe, for their love and support.

Quan Z. Sheng

To my loving wife, Angela, and cherished children, William and Patricia. Your unwavering support fuels each of my endeavours. This book is dedicated to you, my greatest inspirations.

Wei Ni

Contents

Preface...xi

Authors..xiii

List of Figures..xvii

List of Tables...xxi

Chapter 1   Introduction 1

                  1.1   The Essence of Trust Management in an IoV Network..........3
                  1.2   Motivations and Objectives 4
                  1.3   Contributions 4
                  1.4   Book Outline...6

Chapter 2   Literature Review on the Trust Management in the Internet of Vehicles... 10

                  2.1   Overview.. 10
                            2.1.1   Organization of the Chapter..................................... 12
                  2.2   Internet of Vehicles: A Layered Architecture..................... 12
                            2.2.1   Data Source Layer.. 12
                            2.2.2   Edge Layer.. 13
                            2.2.3   Fog Layer.. 13
                            2.2.4   Cloud Layer 13
                  2.3   Towards the Notion of Trust 13
                            2.3.1   Components of Trust.. 14
                            2.3.2   Attributes of Trust.. 14
                            2.3.3   Categories of Trust Management Models 16
                            2.3.4   Categories of Attacks... 17
                            2.3.5   Common Attacks 18
                  2.4   State-of-the-Art Trust Management in IoV 19
                            2.4.1   Conventional Trust Models...................................... 19
                            2.4.2   Bayesian Inference-based Trust Model..................... 22
                            2.4.3   Blockchain-based Trust Model 24
                            2.4.4   Deep/Machine Learning-based Trust Model 25
                            2.4.5   Fuzzy Logic-based Trust Models............................. 27
                            2.4.6   Cryptography-based Trust Model 28
                  2.5   Research Challenges 30
                            2.5.1   Cold Start 30
                            2.5.2   Data Scarcity... 31

		2.5.3	Steady Threshold	31
		2.5.4	Threshold Quantification	31
		2.5.5	Weights Quantification	31
	2.6	Chapter Summary		32

Chapter 3 Context-aware Trust Management for the Internet of Vehicles 39

	3.1	Overview		39
		3.1.1	Safety-critical Applications	39
		3.1.2	Non-safety Applications	40
		3.1.3	Trust Management and Context-awareness	40
		3.1.4	Organization of the Chapter	42
	3.2	Related Work		42
	3.3	Proposed Trust Evaluation and Management for IoV		43
		3.3.1	Local Trust	44
		3.3.2	Context-Dependant Trust	51
		3.3.3	Total Local Trust	52
		3.3.4	Global Trust	53
		3.3.5	Misbehavior Detection	53
	3.4	Simulation Setup and Results		54
	3.5	Chapter Summary		65

Chapter 4 Time-aware Trust Management for the Internet of Vehicles 69

	4.1	Overview		69
		4.1.1	Organization of the Chapter	71
	4.2	Related Work		71
	4.3	System Model		72
	4.4	Simulation Setup and Results		75
		4.4.1	Simulation Setup and Results for TMF2	75
		4.4.2	Simulation Setup and Results for TMF1	81
		4.4.3	Comparison - TMF1 and TMF2	89
	4.5	Chapter Summary		91

Chapter 5 Machine Learning based Trust Management for the Internet of Vehicles..94

	5.1	Overview		94
		5.1.1	Organization of the Chapter	96
	5.2	Related Work		96
	5.3	System Model		97
		5.3.1	Dataset & Feature Extraction	99
		5.3.2	Clustering & Labeling	100
		5.3.3	Classification Model	102
	5.4	Simulation Results		103
		5.4.1	Clustering & Labeling	103

		5.4.2	Classification Model	110
	5.5	Chapter Summary		121
Chapter 6		Conclusion		124
	6.1	Book Summary		124
	6.2	Future Research Directions		127
		6.2.1	Privacy and Trust Management	127
		6.2.2	Data Availability and Trust Management	129

Index **133**

Preface

Over the past few decades, the technological advancements in Vehicular Ad hoc Networks (VANETs) and the Internet of Things (IoT) have brought forth the promising paradigm of the Internet of Vehicles (IoV) which has attracted the attention of numerous researchers from both academia and industry. Today, this promising wireless communication technology plays an indispensable role as vehicles exchange low-latent safety critical messages with one another in a bid to make the road traffic safer, more efficient, and convenient. However, dissemination of malicious messages within the network not only significantly reduces the network performance but also becomes a source of threat for the passengers and the vulnerable pedestrians. Accordingly, a number of trust models have been recently proposed in the literature to ensure the identification and elimination of malicious vehicles from the network. These trust models primarily rely on the aggregation of different trust attributes, e.g., direct and indirect observations, and further evict malicious vehicles based on a particular threshold set on this composite trust value. Nevertheless, quantification of these trust attributes along with the weights associated with them and setting-up of the said threshold pose significant challenges especially owing to diverse influential factors in such a dynamic and distributed networking environment.

Accordingly, this book delineates on the convergence of the notion of trust with the IoV primarily in terms of its underlying rationale. It further sheds some light on the state of the art in the vehicular trust management, IoV architecture, and open challenges in the subject domain. Moreover, multiple unique trust management models have been developed with distinct features and objectives, including, but not limited to, the quantification of influencing trust attributes, quantification of weights affiliated with these attributes, integration of context information, threshold definition, time-variant behavior analysis, and malevolent conduct detection by employing machine learning.

The first major contribution is conducting a comprehensive survey on the state of the art in the vehicular trust management focusing on the essential factors such as quantification of weights, quantification of threshold, misbehavior detection, attack resistance, etc. It further presents an overarching IoV architecture, constituents of the notion of trust, and attacks relating to the IoV in addition to open research challenges in the area of interest.

The second key contribution is proposing a novel trust management mechanism that utilizes context information in addition to employing relevant impacting quantities as weights to formulate trust evaluations. The primary emphasis is the quantification of weights associated with the contributing trust attributes and incorporating (a) attack resilience while constituting certain parameters (i.e., direct and indirect trust) and (b) an adaptive and flexible threshold to mitigate malevolent behavior.

The third significant contribution is analyzing the time-based behavior of the aggregated trust along with the contributing parameters to study the behavior of each vehicle and to identify suitable trust-based patterns for safety-critical and non-safety vehicular applications. Prior to the said analyses, a trust management model has been developed employing a different dataset (i.e., a real IoT dataset) to address the challenges of quantification of the influencing trust attributes and the weights associated with these parameters, subsequently, quantifying the aggregated trust. Later, the time-varying analysis of both trust evaluation frameworks, i.e., the one mentioned in the first contribution and the one indicated in this contribution has been presented.

The fourth main contribution is employing machine learning techniques to mitigate the need (a) to assign weights to the contributing parameters manually and (b) to define an optimal threshold value. It thus computes the feature matrix for four parameters in two different ways, (a) all of the parameters computed by each trustor for a trustee are treated as individual features, and (b) the mean of each single parameter computed by all of the trustors for a trustee is regarded as a collective feature. Different machine learning algorithms were employed for classifying vehicles as trustworthy and untrustworthy.

Sarah Ali Siddiqui
Adnan Mahmood
Quan Z. Sheng
Hajime Suzuki
Wei Ni

Authors

Sarah Ali Siddiqui is a CSIRO Early Research Career (CERC) Fellow in the Cyber Security Automation and Orchestration Team at the Commonwealth Scientific and Industrial Research Organisation (CSIRO)'s, Data61, Australia. She holds a PhD from School of Computing, Macquarie University, Australia, her Masters in Computer Science and Engineering from the University of Jinan, P.R. China, and Bachelors in Electrical (Telecommunications) Engineering from the COMSATS Institute of Information Technology, Islamabad, Pakistan. Sarah has several publications over the years including peer reviewed conference and journal articles, and book chapters. Her most recent publication was in the IEEE Transactions on Intelligent Transportation Systems which is one of the most prestigious venues to publish research on the Internet of Vehicles (IoV) domain. Sarah has also won a number of awards, including, but not limited to, the best thesis, best student paper, student travel grant, CSC scholarship, Data61 PhD top-up scholarship and iMQRES scholarship. Her research interests include Security of Future Networks, Intelligent Transportation Systems, Trust Management, Internet of Vehicles, Machine Learning, and Computer Networks.

Adnan Mahmood possesses a PhD in Computer Science and is a Lecturer in Computing – IoT and Networking at the School of Computing, Macquarie University, Sydney, Australia. Before moving to Macquarie University, Adnan has spent a considerable number of years in both academic and research settings of the Republic of Ireland, Malaysia, Pakistan, and the People's Republic of China. His research interests include, but are not limited to, the Internet of Things (primarily, the Internet of Vehicles), Trust Management, Software-Defined Networking, and the Next Generation Heterogeneous Wireless Networks. Adnan has 70+ publications as refereed book chapters, journal articles, and conference papers with a number of them published in prestigious venues, including, but not limited to, ACM Computing Surveys, IEEE Transactions on Intelligent Transportation Systems, IEEE Transactions on Network and Service Management, ACM Transactions on Sensor Networks, ACM Transactions on Cyber-Physical Systems, and Nature's Scientific Reports. Adnan, besides, serve on the Technical Program Committees of a number of reputed international conferences. He is a member of the IEEE, IET, and the ACM.

Quan Z. (Michael) Sheng is a Distinguished Professor and Head of School of Computing at Macquarie University, Australia. Before moving to Macquarie University, Michael spent 10 years at School of Computer Science, the University of Adelaide, serving in a number of senior leadership roles including interim Head and Deputy Head of School of Computer Science. Michael holds a PhD degree in computer science from the University of New South Wales (UNSW) and did his post-doc as a research scientist at CSIRO ICT Centre. From 1999 to 2001, Michael worked at UNSW as a visiting research fellow. Prior to that, he spent 6 years as a senior software engineer in industries. Prof. Sheng has more than 500 publications as edited books and proceedings, refereed book chapters, and refereed technical papers in journals and conferences. He is ranked by Microsoft Academic as one of the Most Impactful Authors in Services Computing (ranked Top 5 of All Time worldwide) and in the Web of Things (ranked Top 20 All-Time). He is the recipient of the AMiner Most Influential Scholar Award on IoT (2007-2017), ARC (Australian Research Council) Future Fellowship (2014), Chris Wallace Award for Outstanding Research Contribution (2012), and Microsoft Research Fellowship (2003). Prof Michael Sheng is Vice Chair of the Executive Committee of the IEEE Technical Community on Services Computing (IEEE TCSVC) and a member of the ACS (Australian Computing Society) Technical Advisory Board on IoT.

Hajime Suzuki received the B.E. and M.E. degrees from the University of Electro-Communications, Tokyo, Japan, in 1993 and 1995, respectively, and the Ph.D. degree from the University of Technology, Sydney, Australia, in 1999. Since 1999, he has been conducting research and development at the Commonwealth Scientific and Industrial Research Organisation (CSIRO)'s Radiophysics Laboratory in Sydney, Australia. He is currently a Principal Research Scientist at the Cybersecurity & Quantum Systems Group, Software and Computational Systems Research Program, Data61. He is an active participant of the Australian Radio Communication Study Group 3 and of the Study Group 3 (Radio Propagation), International Telecommunication Union Radiocommunication Sector (ITU-R), particularly, of the Working Party 3K (point-to-area propagation). He is currently a Vice Chairman of Working Party 3K.

Wei Ni received the B.E. and Ph.D. degrees in Communication Science and Engineering from Fudan University, Shanghai, China, in 2000 and 2005, respectively. He was a Post-Doctoral Research Fellow at Shanghai Jiao Tong University from 2005 to 2008, the Deputy Project Manager of the Bell Laboratories, Alcatel/Alcatel-Lucent, from 2005 to 2008, and a Senior Researcher with Devices Research and Development, Nokia, from 2008 to 2009. He is currently a Principal Research Scientist at the Commonwealth Scientific and Industrial Research Organisation (CSIRO), a Technical Expert at Standards Australia, a Conjoint Professor at the University of New South Wales, an Adjunct Professor at the University of Technology Sydney, and an Honorary Professor at Macquarie University. He is a Fellow of IEEE. Dr Ni's research interests include security and privacy, machine learning, modelling, and optimization. He has proposed and led significant research projects on aircraft safety and situational awareness, underground mining safety tracking, subterranean robotic challenge, and 6G security and privacy funded by Boeing, Australian Department of Home Affairs, and other government departments. He has authored eight book chapters, more than 300 journal articles, 100 conference papers, 26 patents, and ten standard proposals accepted by IEEE, and contributed to ISO standardisation. He has won several research awards, including the 2022 IEEE IWCMC Best Paper Award, the 2022 Elsevier Best Review Paper Award, and the 2021 Elsevier YJNCA Best Review Paper Award, as well as the 2021 IEEE Vehicular Technology Society (VTS) Chapter of the Year Award. Dr. Ni has served first as the Secretary, Vice-Chair, and then Chair for IEEE New South Wales (NSW) VTS Chapter from 2015 to 2024, the Track Chair for VTC-Spring 2017, the Track Co-Chair for IEEE VTC-Spring 2016, the Publication Chair for BodyNet 2015, and the Student Travel Grant Chair for WPMC 2014. He has been an Editor of IEEE Transactions on Wireless Communications since 2018, an Editor of IEEE Transactions on Vehicular Technology since 2022, and an Editor of IEEE Communications Surveys and Tutorials and IEEE Transactions on Information Forensics and Security since 2024.

List of Figures

1.1 An Overview of Vehicle-to-Everything Communication in an IoV Land-scape. (Please note that the figure in the digital edition is displayed with color.) 2

2.1 A Layered Architecture of an IoV Network. (Please note that the figure in the digital edition is displayed with color.) 12

2.2 Direct and Indirect Trust. (Please note that the figure in the digital edition is displayed with color.) 15

2.3 Attacks in the Internet of Vehicles. (Please note that the figure in the digital edition is displayed with color.) 20

3.1 Context: Safety-critical and Non-safety (Infotainment) Applications. (Please note that the figure in the digital edition is displayed with color.) 41

3.2 System Architecture 45

3.3 Detailed System Framework 46

3.4 Illustration of the Simulator for the IoV Dataset. (Please note that the figure in the digital edition is displayed with color.) 55

3.5 Effect – Packet Delivery Ratio and Direct Trust (Trustee 2 and Trustee 6 at Time 5). (Please note that the figure in the digital edition is displayed with color.) 55

3.6 Comparison – Direct Observation with/without Time Decay (Trustee 2 and Trustee 6 at Time 5). (Please note that the figure in the digital edition is displayed with color.) 56

3.7 Comparison – Global Trust with/without Forgetting Factor (Trustee 2 and Trustee 6). (Please note that the figure in the digital edition is displayed with color.) 57

3.8 Effect of Context – Trust for Safety-critical Communication (Trustee 2 and Trustee 6 at Time 5). (Please note that the figure in the digital edition is displayed with color.) 58

3.9 Effect of Delay – Trust for Safety-critical Communication (Trustee 2). (Please note that the figure in the digital edition is displayed with color.) 59

3.10 Heat Maps – (a) Global Trust with Context, (b) Global Trust without Context, and (c) Residual map – Global Trust with/without Context. (Please note that the figure in the digital edition is displayed with color.) 60

3.11 Comparison of Aggregated Trust – Employing BTCMV, Benchmark, and the Proposed Trust Evaluation Schemes. (Please note that the figure in the digital edition is displayed with color.) 61

3.12 Comparison of Aggregated Trust BTCMV – Employing predefined vis-
à-vis Proposed Weights. (Please note that the figure in the digital edition
is displayed with color.) 63
3.13 Comparison – Steady Threshold vis-à-vis Proposed Adaptive Threshold.
(Please note that the figure in the digital edition is displayed with color.) 66

4.1   Time-varying Patterns for Trust, Familiarity, and Packet Delivery Ratio
of all 76 Vehicles with respect to Percentage Recent Interactions (red
color represents vehicle no. 3, magenta color represents vehicle no. 32,
whereas green color represents vehicle no. 49). (Please note that the fig-
ure in the digital edition is displayed with color.) 76
4.2   Time-varying Patterns for Trust ascertained via Envisaged Scheme vis-
á-vis Trust-based Benchmark Schemes, i.e., Assigning Equal Weights to
the Contributing Parameters (red color represents vehicle no. 3, magenta
color represents vehicle no. 32, whereas green color represents vehicle
no. 49). (Please note that the figure in the digital edition is displayed with
color.) 79
4.3   Aggregated Trust Variation over Time for a) Vehicle no. 33, b) Vehicle
no. 48, and c) Vehicle no. 51. (Please note that the figure in the digital
edition is displayed with color.) 81
4.4   Time-varying Patterns for Global Trust, Direct Trust, Indirect Trust, and
Context Dependent Trust of all 10 Vehicles with respect to Percentage
Recent Interactions (red color represents vehicle no. 1, magenta color
represents vehicle no. 5, whereas green color represents vehicle no. 10).
(Please note that the figure in the digital edition is displayed with color.) 82
4.5   Time-varying Patterns for Direct Trust, Packet Delivery Ratio, and Forgetting Factor of all 10 Vehicles with respect to Percentage Recent Interactions (red color represents vehicle no. 1, magenta color represents
vehicle no. 5, whereas green color represents vehicle no. 10). (Please
note that the figure in the digital edition is displayed with color.) 86
4.6   Time-varying Patterns for Indirect Trust, Neighbor Trust, and Confidence Factor of all 10 Vehicles with respect to Percentage Recent Interactions (red color represents vehicle no. 1, magenta color represents
vehicle no. 5, whereas green color represents vehicle no. 10). (Please
note that the figure in the digital edition is displayed with color.) 88
4.7   Time-varying Patterns for Context Dependent Trust, and Propagation
Delay of all 10 Vehicles with respect to Percentage Recent Interactions
(red color represents vehicle no. 1, magenta color represents vehicle no.
5, whereas green color represents vehicle no. 10). (Please note that the
figure in the digital edition is displayed with color.) 90
4.8   Global Trust Variation over Time for a) Vehicle no. 3, b) Vehicle no. 7,
and c) Vehicle no. 9. (Please note that the figure in the digital edition is
displayed with color.) 91

5.1 Clustering for Labels using Unsupervised Learning for Packet Delivery Ratio vs. Familiarity for vehicles 1 – 6 (The cluster in blue represents *untrustworthy* vehicles whereas the cluster in red depicts *trustworthy* vehicles). (Please note that the figure in the digital edition is displayed with color.) 104

5.2 Clustering for Labels using Unsupervised Learning for Packet Delivery Ratio vs. Timeliness for vehicles 1 – 6 (The cluster in blue represents *untrustworthy* vehicles whereas the cluster in red depicts *trustworthy* vehicles). (Please note that the figure in the digital edition is displayed with color.) 105

5.3 Clustering for Labels using Unsupervised Learning for Packet Delivery Ratio vs. Interaction Frequency for vehicles 1 – 6 (The cluster in blue represents *untrustworthy* vehicles whereas the cluster in red depicts *trustworthy* vehicles). (Please note that the figure in the digital edition is displayed with color.) 106

5.4 Clustering for Labels using Unsupervised Learning for Familiarity vs. Timeliness for vehicles 1 – 6 (The cluster in blue represents *untrustworthy* vehicles whereas the cluster in red depicts *trustworthy* vehicles). (Please note that the figure in the digital edition is displayed with color.) ... 107

5.5 Clustering for Labels using Unsupervised Learning for Familiarity vs. Interaction Frequency for vehicles 1 – 6 (The cluster in blue represents *untrustworthy* vehicles whereas the cluster in red depicts *trustworthy* vehicles). (Please note that the figure in the digital edition is displayed with color.) 108

5.6 Clustering for Labels using Unsupervised Learning for Timeliness vs. Interaction Frequency for vehicles 1 – 6 (The cluster in blue represents *untrustworthy* vehicles whereas the cluster in red depicts *trustworthy* vehicles). (Please note that the figure in the digital edition is displayed with color.) 109

5.7 Clustering for Labels using Unsupervised Learning a) Packet Delivery Ratio vs. Familiarity, b) Packet Delivery Ratio vs. Timeliness, c) Packet Delivery Ratio vs. Interaction Frequency, d) Familiarity vs. Timeliness, e) Familiarity vs. Interaction Frequency, and f) Timeliness vs. Interaction Frequency (The cluster in blue represents *untrustworthy* vehicles whereas the cluster in red depicts *trustworthy* vehicles). (Please note that the figure in the digital edition is displayed with color.) 111

5.8 Decision Boundary for a) Packet Delivery Ratio vs. Familiarity, b) Packet Delivery Ratio vs. Timeliness, c) Packet Delivery Ratio vs. Interaction Frequency, d) Familiarity vs. Timeliness, e) Familiarity vs. Interaction Frequency, and f) Timeliness vs. Interaction Frequency (Boundary for *untrustworthy* vehicles is depicted in blue, whereas, red manifests the *trustworthy* vehicles' region). (Please note that the figure in the digital edition is displayed with color.) 112

5.9   Decision Boundary for Packet Delivery Ratio vs. Familiarity for vehicles
       1 – 6 (Boundary for *untrustworthy* vehicles is depicted in blue, whereas,
       red manifests the *trustworthy* vehicles' region). (Please note that the fig-
       ure in the digital edition is displayed with color.) 113
5.10   Decision Boundary for Packet Delivery Ratio vs. Timeliness for vehicles
       1 – 6 (Boundary for *untrustworthy* vehicles is depicted in blue, whereas,
       red manifests the *trustworthy* vehicles' region). (Please note that the fig-
       ure in the digital edition is displayed with color.) 114
5.11   Decision Boundary for Packet Delivery Ratio vs. Interaction Frequency
       for vehicles 1 – 6 (Boundary for *untrustworthy* vehicles is depicted in
       blue, whereas, red manifests the *trustworthy* vehicles' region). (Please
       note that the figure in the digital edition is displayed with color.) 115
5.12   Decision Boundary for Familiarity vs. Timeliness for vehicles 1 – 6
       (Boundary for *untrustworthy* vehicles is depicted in blue, whereas, red
       manifests the *trustworthy* vehicles' region). (Please note that the figure
       in the digital edition is displayed with color.)... 116
5.13   Decision Boundary for Familiarity vs. Interaction Frequency for vehicles
       1 – 6 (Boundary for *untrustworthy* vehicles is depicted in blue, whereas,
       red manifests the *trustworthy* vehicles' region). (Please note that the fig-
       ure in the digital edition is displayed with color.) 117
5.14   Decision Boundary for Timeliness vs. Interaction Frequency for vehicles
       1 – 6 (Boundary for *untrustworthy* vehicles is depicted in blue, whereas,
       red manifests the *trustworthy* vehicles' region). (Please note that the fig-
       ure in the digital edition is displayed with color.) 118
5.15   Classification Accuracy for Individual Parametric Scores using Different
       Machine Learning Classifiers. (Please note that the figure in the digital
       edition is displayed with color.)... 119
5.16   Classification Accuracy for Mean Parametric Scores using Different Ma-
       chine Learning Classifiers. (Please note that the figure in the digital edi-
       tion is displayed with color.).. 119
5.17   Performance Evaluation of Individual Parametric Scores for Malicious
       Vehicle Classification. (Please note that the figure in the digital edition
       is displayed with color.)... 120
5.18   Performance Evaluation of Mean Parametric Scores for Malicious Ve-
       hicle Classification. (Please note that the figure in the digital edition is
       displayed with color.)... 120

List of Tables

2.1   Comparison of Recent Surveys...11

3.1   Notations & Definitions...47
3.2   A Comparison – Results for Aggregated Trust of Trustee 2 and Trustee 6 – Computed by Employing BTCMV, Benchmark Scheme, and the Proposed Scheme. (Please note that the figure in the digital edition is displayed with color.) 62
3.3   A Comparison – Results for Aggregated Trust of Trustee 2 and Trustee 6 – Computed by BTCMV Employing Predefined Weights to Proposed Weights. 64
3.4   A Comparison of Results for Direct Trust – Computed by RFSN and the Proposed Scheme...65

4.1   Notations & Definitions...73
4.2   Aggregated Trust Trend over Time..78
4.3   Familiarity Trend over Time..80
4.4   Packet Delivery Ratio Trend over Time...80
4.5   Global Trust Trend over Time. 84
4.6   Direct Trust Trend over Time. 84
4.7   Indirect Trust Trend over Time...85
4.8   Context Dependent Trust Trend over Time. 85
4.9   Packet Delivery Ratio Trend over Time...87
4.10 Forgetting Factor Trend over Time..87
4.11 Neighbor Trust Trend over Time. 89
4.12 Confidence Factor Trend over Time. 91
4.13 Propagation Delay Trend over Time..91

5.1   Classification Groups...98
5.2   Notations & Definitions...98

1 Introduction

The evolving needs and growing mobility demands have resulted in an exponential increase in the number of cars on the road [1]. The number of registered road vehicles in Australia alone was recorded to be 20.1 million as of January 2021, according to the Australian Bureau of Statistics [2], and the number of vehicles on the road globally is anticipated to reach up to 2.8 billion by 2036 [3]. Owing to the same, several issues, including, but not limited to, traffic congestion and road accidents have transpired. According to the World Health Organization, the major cause of mortality among the population aged 5–29 years is via road accidents and the number of fatalities is estimated to be about 3,700 people daily whereas the total number of road fatalities is nearly 1.3 million every year, globally [4, 5]. This creates a high demand for innovative and sophisticated traffic management systems. The continued expansion and advancements in connected vehicles are revolutionizing the notion of transportation by further enhancing the intelligent transportation systems (ITS) to improve traffic throughput and road safety by reducing traffic congestion and the risk of road accidents [6, 7]. These systems rely on acquisition, analysis, and processing of the immense volume of sensor data associated with the embedded sensors in modern vehicles. These sensors exchange information with other internal sensors and sensors in their immediate ambience, utilizing the notion of the Internet of Things (IoT), wherein the interconnecting devices exchange data about themselves and their surroundings to form intelligent networks [8]. It is estimated that about 152,200 IoT devices will be connecting to the Internet per minute, subsequently, increasing the data volume up to 73.1 ZB in 2025 [9, 10]. Furthermore, a single car has nearly 100 sensors embedded, and according to a recent estimate, it can generate approximately 380 TB–4.9 PB of data annually [11]. The information shared among the on-board sensors (e.g., position, speed/velocity, pressure, temperature sensors, etc.) and IoT devices (e.g., traffic speed and density sensors, road cameras, etc.) assists in real-time traffic management by creating a true perception of the road and the traffic network [12].

Over the past few decades, researchers from both academia and industry have invested great efforts into technological advancements of mobile ad hoc networks (MANETs), wherein mobile devices create on the fly, self-organizing, and dynamic networks by communicating with one another without any communication infrastructure [13, 14, 15, 16]. MANETs evolved over time and one of the advanced flavors of it, vehicular ad hoc networks (VANETs), were introduced, wherein peer vehicles share information with one another [17, 18]. VANETs hold paramount importance in alleviating traffic related issues in urban areas. The amalgamation of cloud and edge computing with big data and the Internet of Things (IoT) is impelling the evolution of VANETs to bring forth the notion of the Internet of Vehicles (IoV) [19]. Smart connected vehicles relying on Vehicle-to-Everything (V2X) communications aid in providing safe and efficacious traffic flows, subsequently, supporting

DOI: 10.1201/9781032723662-1

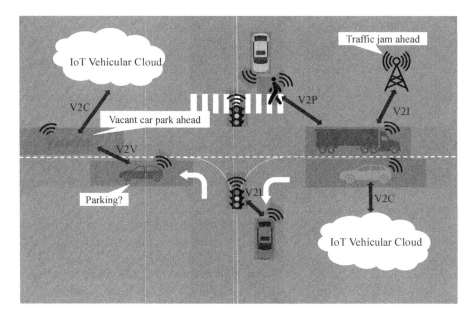

Figure 1.1 An Overview of Vehicle-to-Everything Communication in an IoV Landscape. (Please note that the figure in the digital edition is displayed with color.)

next-generation road mobility and transport [20]. V2X communications encompass vehicle-to-vehicle (V2V), vehicle-to-infrastructure (V2I), vehicle-to-sensor (V2S), vehicle-to-pedestrian (V2P), and vehicle-to-cloud (V2C) communications [21] as illustrated in Fig. 1.1, wherein vehicles utilize wireless media to exchange information with other vehicles, surrounding infrastructure, on-board sensors, personal devices, and the cloud computing environment [22, 23]. The V2X based application scenarios generally include: 1) safety-critical applications, e.g., road congestion, crash avoidance, and collision notification, 2) non-safety applications, e.g., navigation, anti-theft, and 3) entertainment [22]. The V2X communication coupled with the aforementioned sensor embedded vehicles' capabilities helps improve traffic management and road safety by generating collision warnings, emergency brake notifications, hazard warnings, obstacle warning, and traffic congestion warnings [24]. Due to the sensitive nature of these applications, it is crucial that the exchanged information is secure and reliable. However, such messages are vulnerable to attacks where dishonest vehicles can counterfeit safety messages and introduce delays in the transmission resulting in accidents and loss of human lives [25].

The ever-evolving topology owing to the highly mobile nature of vehicular networks, decentralized architecture, pervasive operation, and open infrastructure make it challenging to ensure security and make vehicular networks vulnerable to both insider and outsider attacks [26, 27]. A comprehensive review of the literature demonstrates that numerous cryptography-based security solutions have been suggested, however, these techniques alone have only been proven useful with outsider attacks, wherein the attackers are not authorized users of the network [28]. To tackle insider attacks on vehicular networks, the notion of trust has lately been introduced and several trust management models have been proposed [29]. Trust is defined as the belief of a vehicle (referred to as a trustor) in its peer vehicle (referred to as a trustee) relying on the past interactions among the two and the opinions towards a trustee, acquired by a trustor's neighboring vehicles.

1.1 THE ESSENCE OF TRUST MANAGEMENT IN AN IOV NETWORK

As indicated earlier, vehicular networks are highly vulnerable to attacks due to their high mobility and dynamicity where malicious vehicles can disseminate counterfeited safety-critical messages and interpose unnecessary delays in the communication, consequently causing road accidents and loss of precious human lives. As vehicular networks are becoming even more open access, it is critical to avail the services of the advanced ITS framework with due caution and suspicion as the unrestricted access makes them more susceptible to attacks. These attacks can be classified as insider attacks, outsider attacks, active attacks, passive attacks, etc. Moreover, the anxiety of private data being breached and misused is also experienced by the network users [30]. It is, therefore, of paramount importance that the vehicles receiving messages, i.e., both safety-critical and non-safety (infotainment) messages, from other vehicles, are absolutely positive about the character of the sender as well as the information itself, and it is indispensable that any dishonest vehicles are identified and eliminated before they have an opportunity to cause any damages to the network. For instance, imagine how injurious it would be if a malicious vehicle alters a collision avoidance warning message alerting a vehicle of an impending crash along its path leading to a fatal accident and loss of human lives [31].

Traditional security solutions may not be able to address the aforementioned issues in entirety and offer considerable defence in certain IoV scenarios, e.g., the evaluation of information quality, anonymous authentication, reliability of the data originator, detection and identification of attacks, eradication of misbehaving nodes [30]. Cryptographic techniques have been extensively employed to mitigate dishonest behavior from a vehicular network; however, such solutions alone cannot assist with credibility evaluation of authenticated nodes and are effective only for outside attackers, where the malicious vehicle is not a legitimate member of the network. It is suggested that the traditional security demands, e.g., confidentiality, integrity, authentication, availability of the network needs to be fulfilled. In addition, supplementary measures can be included based on the IoV needs in a specific scenario, e.g., auditing for information tracking, and trustworthiness [30]. With an intent to alleviate insider attackers, the notion of trust, in addition to these cryptography-based techniques, is brought forward where vehicles assess their fellow network participants and the quality of the information originated by them depending on certain communication and physical parameters, including, but not limited to, packet delivery ratio, direct and indirect observations, reputation, familiarity, timeliness, and distance [32].

Trust management specifies a group of steps taken to minimize the harmful effects of misbehaving nodes, i.e., selfish as well as malicious nodes. These nodes are often, collectively, known as dishonest or misbehaving entities; however, it is important to learn the difference among the two. A node that intentionally harm the network, i.e., by dispersing counterfeited or altered information, is referred to as a malicious node while the nodes that restrict their interaction with others to conserve their resources are known as selfish nodes. The trust-based models aid in preventing dissemination of altered and falsified information along with the eradication of the vehicles generating such messages, thereby, guaranteeing safe and efficacious traffic flows. These trust management models are classified into (i) data-centric, where the accuracy of the disseminated data is of primary interest; (ii) entity-centric, where the credibility of the message originating vehicle is the main focus; and (iii) hybrid, where the authenticity of both the information and the source vehicle is emphasized.

1.2   MOTIVATIONS AND OBJECTIVES

The development of trust-based vehicular security models helps avoid the exchange of counterfeited or altered safety-critical messages and further assists in eliminating dishonest vehicles disseminating such falsified data by assessing data/information-centric and entity/node-centric trust values attributed to influencing trust parameters in order to ensure road safety. These trust attributes are translated into numerical values by formulating them in terms of communication and network characteristics. Subsequently, it helps achieve the overall trust quantification, i.e., the expression of the trustworthiness of a vehicle in the form of a number. Weights, reflecting significance of each of the trust parameters, are associated with corresponding parameters while accumulating the overall trust score. Moreover, a minimum acceptable trust score, termed as threshold, is generally pre-defined to classify vehicles as trustworthy or dishonest according to their respective computed trust scores. Nevertheless, formulating the trust parameters, and determining the values of their associated weights and that of the threshold with greater precision is exceptionally complicated. Furthermore, it is especially important to consider and tackle trust-based attacks while formulating the contributing trust parameters.

In light of the above, the aim of the research-at-hand is to explore the possibility of designing a scalable trust management model to cope with the problems of effective weights and optimal threshold selection in vehicular networks. The research-at-hand has the potential to significantly revolutionize the transportation sector within the next few years by improving the road safety thereby strengthening the emerging paradigm of futuristic smart cities. Enabling the vehicles to efficaciously exchange safety messages results in making road travel safer, and in turn, decreases the number of road fatalities which currently are significantly high [33, 34].

1.3   CONTRIBUTIONS

Whilst the existing literature has already demonstrated some significant contributions in securing vehicular networks, nevertheless, they still lack the potential of being generic enough to be commonly applied to any service domain and across diverse parameters. Moreover, the existing research studies only rely on the conventional factors in the trust assessment process and the impact of certain influential indicators on the trust assessment, the aggregation process, and the identification of misbehaving vehicles have been completely overlooked.

In light of the above, the proposed work intends to address the following open issues in order to implement state-of-the-art vehicular trust management models for diverse road safety applications and services:

1. How to devise a context aware trust management framework to ascertain the dynamic nature of vehicular networks via conventional mechanisms?

   Trust management models primarily rely on aggregating trust components, e.g., direct trust and indirect trust, in order to compute a single trust metric of a particular vehicle. Direct trust is generally a vehicle's direct observation about the target vehicle, whereas, indirect trust encompasses the opinions of the neighboring vehicles pertinent to the target vehicle. Weights need to be assigned according to the significance of individual direct observations, preference of the neighbor's opinion in indirect trust and the precedence of feature parameters. However, assigning of these weights involves complex issues as it is extremely difficult to quantify these weights and for which complex computation is indispensable. Moreover, a steady threshold value is often set manually to identify trusted vehicles in the vehicular network/cluster, i.e., a vehicle having the Trust Value higher than the threshold is considered a trusted vehicle whereas the vehicles with a trust value below the predefined threshold are categorized as dishonest vehicles. However, defining a steady threshold does not cater to the network dynamics of ever changing vehicular networks. In addition, while formulating individual contributing trust parameters, it is of significance to cater to the attack prone nature of the vehicular networks. Furthermore, the information concerning safety-critical and non-safety (infotainment) applications needs to be incorporated to ensure rigorous criterion while evaluating trust scores to meet the stringent demands of these vehicular applications [35].

2. How to analyze time-varying trends of trust assigned to vehicles in an IoV networks to study the behavior and suitability of vehicles for specific applications (i.e., safety-critical and non-safety)?

   Time-varying analysis helps understand and estimate patterns of complex relationships among participating quantities. Moreover, it supports studying the behavior of each vehicle to identify suitable trust-based patterns for safety-critical and non-safety vehicular applications. Vehicular safety-critical applications such as collision warning, emergency brake notification and traffic congestion warning demand sensitivity to real-time performance, whereas, non-safety applications such as locating fuel stations, Internet services and location prediction services make use of the overall performance patterns of the nodes. Extensive research has been performed on the steady-state analysis, however, time-varying trends need further investigation [36].

3. How to accurately and intuitively aggregate influencing trust parameters, and classify dishonest vehicles via learning mechanisms in order to mitigate the need to assign weights and define misbehavior detection threshold?

Quantification of manual weights associated to contributing trust attributes gets complicated when the number of such attributes is large. Moreover, as mentioned previously, selecting an optimal value for the misbehavior detection is crucial as deciding a lower value for threshold can result in severe damage caused by the malicious vehicles before they are finally evicted as the trust values take some time to drop down to a lower value whereas setting it too high will lead to the removal of legitimate and honest vehicles as well due to a momentary slip. Learning techniques are significantly important in deciding the weights and decision boundary without having to formulate these manually [37, 38].

1.4 BOOK OUTLINE

Chapter 2 covers the Background on IoV with a discussion on IoV architecture, the concept of trust and its constituents, and IoV attacks. It further offers a comprehensive review of the state-of-the-art trust management employing diverse computational domains, including, but not limited to, machine learning, Bayesian inference, blockchain and fuzzy logic. Moreover a comparison in respect of the evaluation tools, quantification of weights, misbehavior detection, attack resistance, and quantification of threshold is also presented. Finally, the open research challenges in the existing literature on vehicular network security have also been included.

Chapter 3 presents an overview of the existing state-of-the-art trust management models in vehicular networks inline with the targeted research problem. It further discusses the system architecture and the mathematical modelling of the proposed trust management framework in depth. Moreover, the simulation setup and experimental results have been presented prior to the concluding remarks.

Chapter 4 provides a comprehensive glimpse into the existing literature of trust management in vehicular networks aligned with the focused research question, i.e., with respect to weight quantification and time-varying behavioral analysis. The details regarding the formulation of trust parameters for the proposed trust management scheme have been further described in the chapter. Moreover a thorough time-based analysis preceded by a detailed discussion on the simulation results has also been included followed by the closing comments.

Chapter 5 sheds light on the existing literature employing different computational mechanisms for trust management and misbehavior detection in vehicular networks. Furthermore, the discussion on mathematical formulation for feature extraction has also been presented. Subsequently, unsupervised learning has been utilized for labelling purposes of an IoT dataset prior to applying supervised learning algorithms for classification of vehicles into trustworthy and untrustworthy categories while avoiding the introduction of manual weights as well as pre-defined steady threshold.

It further provides a detailed analysis of simulation results followed by the concluding comments.

Chapter 6 includes the concluding remarks of the research-at-hand followed by the open research challenges for prospective research.

REFERENCES

1. S. Wei, Y. Zou, X. Zhang, T. Zhang, and X. Li. *An Integrated Longitudinal and Lateral Vehicle Following Control System with Radar and Vehicle-to-Vehicle Communication.* IEEE Transactions on Vehicular Technology 68(2), 1116 (2019).
2. *Australian Bureau of Statistics, "Motor Vehicle Census, Australia," June 2021.* https://www.abs.gov.au/statistics/industry/tourism-and-transport/motor-Vehicle-census-australia/latest-release#key-statistics. Accessed: 2024-01-15.
3. *How many Cars are there in the World?* https://www.carsguide.com.au/car-advice/how-many-cars-are-there-in-the-world-70629. Accessed: 2024-01-15.
4. *Road Traffic Injuries.* https://www.who.int/news-room/fact-sheets/detail/road-traffic-injuries. Accessed: 2024-01-15.
5. *Association for Safe International Road Traffic.* https://www.asirt.org/safe-travel/road-safety-facts/. Accessed: 2024-01-15.
6. R. Miucic. *Connected Vehicles: Intelligent Transportation Systems* (Springer, 2018).
7. J. Oncken and B. Chen. *Real-time Model Predictive Powertrain Control for a Connected Plug-in Hybrid Electric Vehicle.* IEEE Transactions on Vehicular Technology 69(8), 8420 (2020).
8. W. E. Zhang, Q. Z. Sheng, A. Mahmood, M. Zaib, S. A. Hamad, A. Aljubairy, A. A. F. Alhazmi, S. Sagar, C. Ma, et al. *The 10 Research Topics in the Internet of Things.* In *2020 IEEE 6th International Conference on Collaboration and Internet Computing (CIC),* pp. 34–43 (IEEE, 2020).
9. *Internet of Things Statistics for 2021 – Taking Things Apart.* https://dataprot.net/statistics/iot-statistics/. Accessed: 2024-01-15.
10. *IDC Forecasts Connected IoT Devices to Generate 79.4ZB of Data in 2025.* https://futureiot.tech/idc-forecasts-connected-iot-devices-to-generate-79-4zb-of-data-in-2025/. Accessed: 2024-01-15.
11. *Autonomous Cars Generate more than 300 TB of Data per Year.* https://www.tuxera.com/blog/autonomous-cars-300-tb-of-data-per-year/. Accessed: 2024-01-15.
12. P. Arthurs, L. Gillam, P. Krause, N. Wang, K. Halder, and A. Mouzakitis. *A Taxonomy and Survey of Edge Cloud Computing for Intelligent Transportation Systems and Connected Vehicles.* IEEE Transactions on Intelligent Transportation Systems (2021).
13. P. Ruiz and P. Bouvry. *Survey on Broadcast Algorithms for Mobile Ad Hoc Networks.* ACM Computing Surveys (CSUR) 48(1), 1 (2015).
14. J.-H. Cho, A. Swami, and R. Chen. *A Survey on Trust Management for Mobile Ad Hoc Networks.* IEEE Communications Surveys & Tutorials 13(4), 562 (2010).
15. F. Aftab, Z. Zhang, and A. Ahmad. *Self-Organization based Clustering in MANETs using Zone based Group Mobility.* IEEE Access 5, 27464 (2017).
16. S. K. Das, K. Kant, and N. Zhang. *Handbook on Securing Cyber-Physical Critical Infrastructure* (Elsevier, 2012).
17. S. A. Alfadhli, S. Lu, A. Fatani, H. Al-Fedhly, and M. Ince. *SD2PA: A Fully Safe Driving and Privacy-preserving Authentication Scheme for VANETs.* Human-centric Computing and Information Sciences 10(1), 1 (2020).

18. C. Cooper, D. Franklin, M. Ros, F. Safaei, and M. Abolhasan. *A Comparative Survey of VANET Clustering Techniques*. IEEE Communications Surveys & Tutorials 19(1), 657 (2016).
19. L.-L. Wang, J.-S. Gui, X.-H. Deng, F. Zeng, and Z.-F. Kuang. *Routing Algorithm Based on Vehicle Position Analysis for Internet of Vehicles*. IEEE Internet of Things Journal 7(12), 11701 (2020).
20. Y. Xing, C. Lv, and D. Cao. *Personalized Vehicle Trajectory Prediction based on Joint Time-Series Modeling for Connected Vehicles*. IEEE Transactions on Vehicular Technology 69(2), 1341 (2020).
21. A. Mahmood, W. E. Zhang, and Q. Z. Sheng. *Software-defined Heterogeneous Vehicular Networking: The Architectural Design and Open Challenges*. Future Internet 11(3), 70 (2019).
22. M. Hasan, S. Mohan, T. Shimizu, and H. Lu. *Securing Vehicle-to-Everything (V2X) Communication Platforms*. IEEE Transactions on Intelligent Vehicles 5(4), 693 (2020).
23. M. Sepulcre and J. Gozalvez. *Heterogeneous V2V Communications in Multi-Link and Multi-RAT Vehicular Networks*. IEEE Transactions on Mobile Computing 20(1), 162 (2021).
24. S. Gyawali, S. Xu, Y. Qian, and R. Q. Hu. *Challenges and Solutions for Cellular based V2X Communications*. IEEE Communications Surveys & Tutorials 23(1), 222 (2020).
25. Z. A. Biron, S. Dey, and P. Pisu. *Real-time Detection and Estimation of Denial of Service Attack in Connected Vehicle Systems*. IEEE Transactions on Intelligent Transportation Systems 19(12), 3893 (2018).
26. S. Tangade, S. S. Manvi, and P. Lorenz. *Trust Management Scheme based on Hybrid Cryptography for Secure Communications in VANETs*. IEEE Transactions on Vehicular Technology 69(5), 5232 (2020).
27. M. N. Mejri, J. Ben-Othman, and M. Hamdi. *Survey on VANET Security Challenges and possible Cryptographic Solutions*. Vehicular Communications 1(2), 53 (2014).
28. S. Tangade, S. S. Manvi, and P. Lorenz. *Decentralized and Scalable Privacy-preserving Authentication Scheme in VANETs*. IEEE Transactions on Vehicular Technology 67(9), 8647 (2018).
29. W. Li and H. Song. *ART: An Attack-Resistant Trust Management Scheme for Securing Vehicular Ad Hoc Networks*. IEEE Transactions on Intelligent Transportation Systems 17(4), 960 (2016).
30. A. Hbaieb, S. Ayed, and L. Chaari. *A Survey of Trust Management in the Internet of Vehicles. Computer Networks 203, 108558 (2022).*
31. A. Mahmood, Q. Z. Sheng, S. A. Siddiqui, S. Sagar, W. E. Zhang, H. Suzuki, and W. Ni. *When Trust Meets the Internet of Vehicles: Opportunities, Challenges, and Future Prospects*. In *2021 IEEE 7th International Conference on Collaboration and Internet Computing (CIC)*, pp. 60–67 (IEEE, 2021).
32. S. A. Siddiqui, A. Mahmood, Q. Z. Sheng, H. Suzuki, and W. Ni. *A Survey of Trust Management in the Internet of Vehicles*. Electronics 10(18), 2223 (2021).
33. Z. Lu, Q. Wang, G. Qu, and Z. Liu. *BARS: A Blockchain-based Anonymous Reputation System for Trust Management in VANETs*. In *2018 17th IEEE International Conference On Trust, Security And Privacy in Computing and Communications/12th IEEE International Conference on Big Data Science and Engineering (TrustCom/BigDataSE)*, pp. 98–103 (IEEE, 2018).
34. M. Aloqaily, S. Otoum, I. Al Ridhawi, and Y. Jararweh. *an Intrusion Detection System for Connected Vehicles in Smart Cities*. Ad Hoc Networks 90, 101842 (2019).

35. S. A. Siddiqui, A. Mahmood, Q. Z. Sheng, H. Suzuki, and W. Ni. *Trust in Vehicles: Towards Context-aware Trust and Attack Resistance for the Internet of Vehicles*. IEEE Transactions on Intelligent Transportation Systems 24(9), 9546 (2023).
36. S. A. Siddiqui, A. Mahmood, Q. Z. Sheng, H. Suzuki, and W. Ni. *A Time-aware Trust Management Heuristic for the Internet of Vehicles*. In *2021 IEEE 20th International Conference on Trust, Security and Privacy in Computing and Communications (Trust-Com)*, pp. 1–8 (IEEE, 2021).
37. S. A. Siddiqui, A. Mahmood, W. E. Zhang, and Q. Z. Sheng. *Machine Learning Based Trust Model for Misbehaviour Detection in Internet-of-Vehicles*. In T. Gedeon, K. W. Wong, and M. Lee, eds., *Neural Information Processing*, pp. 512–520 (Springer International Publishing, Cham, 2019).
38. S. A. Siddiqui, A. Mahmood, Q. Z. Sheng, H. Suzuki, and W. Ni. *Towards a Machine Learning Driven Trust Management Heuristic for the Internet of Vehicles*. Sensors 23(4), 2325 (2023).

2 Literature Review on the Trust Management in the Internet of Vehicles

This chapter provides a comprehensive review of the state of the art in the vehicular trust management employing diverse computational domains, including, but not limited to machine learning, Bayesian inference, blockchain, and fuzzy logic, focusing on factors such as quantification of weights, quantification of threshold, misbehavior detection, evaluation tools, and attack resistance. Moreover, an overarching IoV architecture, constituents within the notion of trust, and attacks relating to the IoV have also been presented in addition to open research challenges in the subject domain.

2.1 OVERVIEW

The employment of trust management schemes prevents vehicles from exchanging fake safety messages and help eradicate nodes dispersing counterfeited information by computing data and entity-based trust scores relying on trust attributes to guarantee safe and reliable traffic flows. Weights are assigned to these trust attributes to reflect their respective influence on the trust computation, and a threshold is specified to identify dishonest vehicles based on the calculated trust scores. Defining precise values for the weights associated with the contributing attributes and the steady threshold is extremely challenging. Moreover, it is of considerable importance to evaluate the performance of the envisaged trust management models against diverse attacks by introducing attack specific adversaries. This chapter provides a comprehensive review of the state of the art in vehicular trust management employing diverse computational domains, including, but not limited to, Bayesian inference, blockchain, machine learning, and fuzzy logic. Furthermore, the review presents a comparison among the said trust management models in respect of the evaluation tools, quantification of weights, misbehavior detection, attack resistance, and quantification of threshold. Table 2.1 presents a comparison of the recently published surveys on the vehicular trust management vis-à-vis the published survey based on this chapter. The table depicts that the recently published surveys do not account for the trust aggregation process (i.e., the trust attributes and the quantification of weights associated with them) and lack the discussion on the computational methodologies employed for trust evaluation. Considering these challenges, we summarize the salient contributions of this chapter as follows:

- We provide an overarching background of the IoV architecture along with a comprehensive discussion on the notion of trust (and its indispensable constituents) and some major attacks that can transpire on an IoV network;

Table 2.1 Comparison of Recent Surveys.

Ref.	Title	Methodology based	Misbehavior detection	Trust Aggregation	Salient Contributions
[1]	Trust Management for Vehicular Networks: An Adversary-oriented Overview	✗	✓	✗	Adversary-oriented survey; discussion on cryptography, trust based solutions, and attacks that can overpower both.
[2]	A Survey on Recent Advances in Vehicular Network Security, Trust, and Privacy	✗	✓	✗	Background on VANETs; discussion on security services, location privacy protection schemes, and simulators; review of authentication schemes; analysis of trust management models.
[3]	Trust in VANET: A Survey of Current Solutions and Future Research Opportunities	✓	~	✗	Comprehensive review on vehicular trust management; description of attack mitigation employing the said trust management mechanisms.
[4]	A Survey of Trust Management in the Internet of Vehicles	✓	✓	✓	Background on IoV; discussion on IoV architecture, trust and its constituents, and IoV attacks; comprehensive review of the state-of-the-art trust management employing diverse computational domains; comparison in respect of the evaluation tools, quantification of weights, misbehavior detection, attack resistance, and quantification of threshold; open research challenges.

✗ Not Addressed, ~ Partially Addressed, ✓ Addressed.

- We review the state of the art in the vehicular trust management with a focus on some key factors, including, but not limited to, quantification of weights, quantification of threshold, and misbehavior detection;
- We identify and subsequently discuss the open research challenges in the subject domain.

2.1.1 ORGANIZATION OF THE CHAPTER

The rest of this chapter is organized as follows: Section 2.2 provides necessary background of the IoV architecture. Section 2.3 discusses the notion of trust and its constituents. Section 2.4 presents a comprehensive review of the existing state-of-the-art trust management models. Section 2.5 discusses the open challenges in the subject domain. Finally, Section 2.6 offers concluding remarks.

2.2 INTERNET OF VEHICLES: A LAYERED ARCHITECTURE

The layered hierarchy of the Internet of Vehicles is similar to that of the Internet of Things as smart vehicles are connected to other vehicles and smart infrastructure to share data over the Internet. Figure 2.1 depicts the layered IoV architecture.

2.2.1 DATA SOURCE LAYER

Nearly 100 sensors are embedded in modern vehicles, and it is anticipated that these sensors will increase to approximately double in number expeditiously [5]. These diverse sensors acquire data from the immediate ambience of the vehicle, which

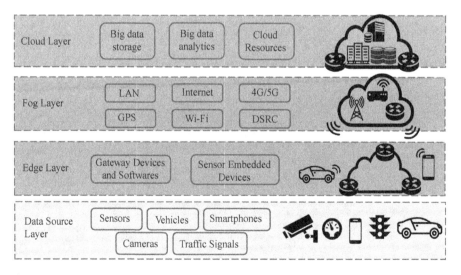

Figure 2.1 A Layered Architecture of an IoV Network. (Please note that the figure in the digital edition is displayed with color.)

combined with the information gathered by V2V, V2I, and V2P communications belong to the data source layer. Due to the limited processing capability of a vehicle, only a limited volume of these data are processed at this layer.

2.2.2   EDGE LAYER

Owing to the critical nature of the vehicles' and traffic related information, the processing and analysis of the immense volume of the data gathered by the sensors and V2X communications need to be achieved in real-time. Accordingly, an edge layer is introduced to further process such data without incurring the cloud-related delays by utilizing the same sensor embedded smart vehicles, infrastructure or gateway devices.

2.2.3   FOG LAYER

This layer, just like the edge layer, is introduced to reduce the dependence on cloud for data analysis. The fog layer accomplishes further processing of data at a local level utilizing intermediate networking infrastructure, V2I communications, Wi-Fi, LAN, etc., consequently, ensuring prompt decision-making and preventing latency issues which might have transpired by relying only on cloud for all the processing [6].

2.2.4   CLOUD LAYER

This layer encompasses big data storage and cloud servers for storage and extensive computation of the massive volume of data which cannot be processed at the preceding layers. Due to the latency issues introduced by the cloud, the data that is not critical for expeditious decision-making, e.g., data required for high-end applications such as traffic navigation systems and traffic flow monitoring systems, is analyzed on this layer.

Vehicular networks are susceptible to attacks due to the dynamic topology and high mobility. To prevent the vehicular networks against the insider attacks, the notion of trust is introduced.

2.3   TOWARDS THE NOTION OF TRUST

Most experts, irrespective of domain, conceptualize trust as a certain degree of risk, vulnerability, or uncertainty, and it establishes an expectation regarding the way an entity might behave in future [7]. Trust is a multifarious abstraction which relies entirely on the subject's perceptive. In psychology, trust is often defined as the degree of likelihood of an individual's anticipation/expectation towards another (i.e., a peer) with regards to the peer's conduct on which one's welfare relies [8, 9]. Trusting reflects the belief of a trustor that the trustee will not exploit the trustor for its (i.e., the trustee's) benefit, the trustee will not exhibit malicious behavior towards the trustor and is inclined to sacrifice for the trustor, and that the trustee is capable of acting for the benefit of the trustor [9, 10]. In sociology, it is believed that reciprocity and cooperation in social interactions or voluntary associations derive trust [11]. In economics, having confidence on the business associates' reliability and integrity, and on the transactions among them is defined as trust. Furthermore, given the nature of online businesses with no physical interaction among the trading parties and with the products, trust plays a significant role in reducing risks associated with business transactions and information asymmetry, and allows acclaimed sellers to achieve price premiums [8, 12].

Trust, as a tactic to enhance the security, has been used with a variety of interpretations by researchers in computer science. It is said to be the belief of a trustor on the reliability of a target node with an aim to achieve a trust objective under certain conditions [13]. In other words, trust is the perception of an evaluator regarding the character, relying on past interactions with a target entity and/or the opinions of the trustworthy nodes [14]. We define trust as the confidence of a trustor towards a trustee based on the past experiences among the two and the recommendations received from the trustor's neighbors regarding the trustee. Most, if not all, of the trust management models discussed in this chapter are (more or less) using similar definitions of trust.

2.3.1 COMPONENTS OF TRUST

The notion of trust relies on the quality of interactions between two entities usually encompassing these components [15]:

Direct Trust: Direct trust exhibits the direct observations of a trustor on a target vehicle, relying on the interactions among the two [16]. Some researchers use the term knowledge to define the direct information gathered by the trustor to evaluate the trustee utilizing certain parameters relying on the participating nodes and the services [17]. It is believed that the significance of direct trust exceeds the indirect trust, however; the amalgamation of both is taken into consideration while assessing a vehicle [5]. Figure 2.2 delineates direct and indirect trust among vehicles.

Indirect Trust: Indirect trust manifests the opinions of the neighboring/trusted entities of a trustor regarding the target node (trustee), taking into account the past experiences with the node in question. Some researchers use the amalgamation of reputation and experience to explain indirect observation. Reputation accumulates all the past experiences with a target node to depict a global opinion regarding that node, whereas experience is a correlation among the trustor and the trustee relying on the belief of the trustor regarding the degree of confidence on the trustee to carry out a task [13].

2.3.2 ATTRIBUTES OF TRUST

A variety of influencing trust attributes are considered while computing the above-mentioned trust components:

Similarity: Similarity relates to the degree of similar content and services among any two vehicles. In the literature, similarity among the messages or vehicles is often

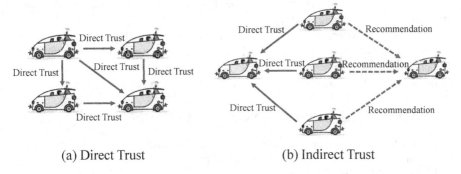

(a) Direct Trust   (b) Indirect Trust

Figure 2.2 Direct and Indirect Trust. (Please note that the figure in the digital edition is displayed with color.)

taken as the Euclidean distance, the direction of movement of two nodes, i.e., cosine similarity, or the positioning-based trajectory similarity [18, 19, 20].

Familiarity: Familiarity manifests how familiar/acquainted two vehicles are with one another. A high familiarity score reflects considerable prior knowledge of the evaluator regarding the trustee. This feature is adapted from social networks where more familiarity leads to a greater level of trust in interpersonal relations [21].

Timeliness: Timeliness delineates how recent the interaction among two vehicles is and it is computed by taking into account the current time instance and the instance when the interaction took place [22]. It is of paramount significance to maintain the timeliness of data and the trust scores, as the outdated information reflects an obsolete trust value that can lead to dire repercussions [23].

Packet Delivery Ratio: The packet delivery ratio is the degree of how well a trustor is connected to the trustee. In the literature, it is often defined as the packet forwarding rate among nodes and is considered as the sole parameter to compute the direct trust towards a trustee. Furthermore, it is also regarded as a primary objective and core criterion while designing trust models and identifying malicious behavior, respectively [23, 24, 25].

Co-Work Relationship: Co-work relationship describes the interactions relying on the services instead of the physical proximity. Analogous to social networks, two nodes exhibit a working association when a node offers a service needed by the other, and it can be computed through a comparison of multicast interactions [26].

Cooperativeness: Cooperativeness defines the willingness of a node to collaborate with its peers for improved network operations. This feature is of great significance to maintain stability in a vehicular network, consequently, incentives are introduced in order to promote cooperative behavior among different vehicles in a network [26, 27, 28].

Duration of Interactions: Duration depicts the length of the interaction among two nodes. It is presumed that considerably long interactions lead to better collaboration among entities which result in development of a much higher trust level. This is because the longer the interaction is, the more an entity can learn regarding the other's conduct and capability [26].

Frequency of Interactions: Frequency is the measure of how often the trustor and the trustee interact with each other. Every time a pair of nodes interact, they get an opportunity to acquire information concerning each other's communication and behavioral patterns which result in more accurate trust computations [26].

2.3.3 CATEGORIES OF TRUST MANAGEMENT MODELS

Vehicular trust management models are generally categorized in three groups, namely data-centric, entity-centric, and hybrid trust management models:

Data-Centric Trust Management Models: This category of trust management models focuses mainly on the accuracy and legitimacy of the information shared among vehicles. This information primarily includes reports and warnings regarding an event. The data-oriented trust models evaluate the honesty of every incident, therefore, delays and data loss may be experienced in case of dense traffic scenarios. Conversely, these trust models do not perform satisfactorily in information sparsity due to the lack of enough evidence. It is believed that in this category, the participating entities do not hold long-term trust associations [5, 14, 29]. Numerous data focused trust management schemes have been proposed in the existing research works, wherein (i) the trust level of the data is assessed by associating weights to the reports (i.e., regarding an event) shared by neighboring vehicles. The associated weights rely on the time and location proximity of a vehicle with regards to the reported event, i.e., a vehicle in the close proximity of an event will have more up-to-date and credible information regarding that event [30], or (ii) the trust level of the message is assessed by considering content conflict and similarity, and the similarity in routing path. Subsequently, a trust value reflecting the probability of the message being authentic is assigned to every exchanged message [31].

Entity-Centric Trust Management Models: This category of trust management models emphasizes on the reliability of the participating vehicle by utilizing the sender's reputation and neighbor recommendations towards it. Therefore, sufficient data is required regarding the originator of the message and its neighboring vehicles for accurate assessment which is rather complicated considering the highly mobile nature of vehicular networks. It is believed that the authenticity of the messages could be an issue as there is no guarantee that the messages originated/sent by the honest vehicles could not be corrupted [14]. Several entity focused trust management schemes have been proposed in the existing research works, wherein (i) the trust score of every vehicle is evaluated amalgamating direct and indirect trust scores prior to electing a cluster head. The vehicle having a trust score greater than a predefined threshold is classified as a trustworthy vehicle, or else, it is categorized as a malicious one [32, 33], or (ii) to prevent the network from selecting a malicious vehicle as the data forwarding agent, an aggregated score for vehicles is computed based on the amalgamation of a vehicle's current level of trustworthiness, its cooperativeness, and the recommendation of the last hop. The highest scoring vehicle is selected as the relay vehicle for data dissemination [34].

Hybrid Trust Management Models: This category of trust management models encompasses both the data and the entity-based trust evaluation, i.e., authenticity of the exchanged data, neighbor's recommendation towards the trustee and its (i.e., trustee's) reputation are taken into account. In other words, the honesty of an event is reflected by the trustworthiness of the sender vehicle. An extensive literature review suggests that numerous hybrid trust management models have been presented, wherein (i) both node and data trust are evaluated and performance is evaluated in the presence of dishonest nodes that counterfeit safety-critical information in addition to advertising false trust rating to deceive the trustworthy vehicles into trusting corrupt information [35], or (ii) both node and data trust are assessed to guarantee reliable data exchange among entities and authenticity of the data disseminated by these entities. The final trust computation aggregates the weighted trust score based on a vehicle's cooperation with its peers, and the weighted trust value reflecting the quality of data sent by the vehicle to its neighbor [36].

2.3.4   CATEGORIES OF ATTACKS

The highly mobile and dynamic nature of the vehicular networks, and the lack of pervasive infrastructure lead to the vulnerability against numerous attacks classified according to their demeanor, nature, and the extent of the damage caused by them. The broad categories of attacks specific to vehicular networks are as follows.

Active Attacks: The attackers in an active attack originate counterfeited messages or alter the contents of legitimate messages. It is rather easy and inexpensive to detect such attacks; however, they are not easy to avoid. The main objective of these attacks is to modify network operations and physical security measures are indispensable to be implemented in this regard [37].

Passive Attacks: Passive attacks are launched to gain insight into the target node without altering the message content. The primary purpose of such attacks is to acquire disseminated data from the network and they are harder to detect as they do not disrupt network operations. In passive attacks, the attackers do not take part in the network communications and encrypting data can help avoid these attacks [37, 38].

Malicious Attacks: Malicious attacks are initiated with a purpose to harm the participating nodes of the network instead of benefiting from the attacks. Such attacks can be awfully destructive and are regarded as extremely dangerous. In some cases, malicious attacker may drop or spread bogus safety-critical information endangering the safety of the drivers, passengers, and pedestrians [39].

Selfish Attacks: Unlike malicious attackers, selfish attackers aim for personal gain from the attack, e.g., to preserve their resources by not relaying the received messages. This indicates a considerably low collaboration rate among vehicles. Incentive-based techniques are often employed to prevent selfish behaviors and encourage cooperation among vehicles [40].

Insider Attacks: Insider attacks are launched by legitimate users of the network, i.e., the users who have already cleared the authentication phase and are a part of the network in question. Due to their knowledge of the network, the attackers are able to launch attacks rather easily. To mitigate such attacks, trust management is introduced in the networks.

Outsider Attacks: In contrast to insider attacks, outsider attacks are executed by nodes that do not have a direct access to the authorized nodes of the network. The attackers do not possess prior knowledge of the network and so these attacks are relatively less damaging. Cryptography-based techniques are often employed to prevent such attacks.

2.3.5 COMMON ATTACKS

Numerous attacks fall under the aforementioned categories of attacks in vehicular networks. Some of the most common attacks belonging to these categories, include but are not limited to, the following attacks:

Man-in-the-Middle Attack: A man-in-the-middle attack occurs when a dishonest vehicle intercepts and/or alters the data exchanged among honest vehicles. The said data may contain safety-critical information, e.g., a blind intersection warning, and altering or counterfeiting such messages threatens the lives of the drivers, passengers, and the pedestrians [41].

Sybil Attack: When a malicious vehicle disrupts the network applications by claiming or stealing multiple identities, the attack is known as a Sybil attack. It can be used to deceive other vehicles into believing that there is a road congestion by showing a higher number of vehicles than actually exists on the road [42].

Bad-Mouthing and Ballot Stuffing Attack: Trust management models employing neighbor recommendations towards the target vehicle as a part of trust computations can fall victim to bad-mouthing attacks. In these attacks, dishonest vehicles collude to harm the reputation of a vehicle by providing unfair negative ratings for it. In ballot stuffing attacks, vehicles assign unfair positive ratings to a target vehicle to boost its reputation [43, 44].

On–Off Attack: Dishonest vehicles do not necessarily depict malicious behavior persistently, instead, there are attackers who behave intelligently, i.e., they switch between honest mode (i.e., where they gain a higher trust score) and dishonest mode (i.e., where they launch an attack). Such attacks are known as on-off attacks and allow the intelligent attackers to cause damage without being tagged and evicted from the vehicular network [5].

Selective Behavior Attack: Analogous to on-off attacks, there might be a case where malicious vehicles behave maliciously (i.e., share counterfeited messages) with some nodes, whereas with other nodes, they behave honestly (i.e., share reliable information). This could result in contradictory trust scores (i.e., based on the direct or/and the indirect observation) assigned to a vehicle by its peers [45].

Black-Hole Attack: Black-hole attackers manipulate other vehicles to transmit data through them (i.e., the attackers) by advertising the route through them (i.e., the attackers) as the best route despite having no route to the desired destination. Once other vehicles send the data to these attackers, they create a blackhole by dropping the data sent towards them [46].

An illustration of Sybil attack, bad-mouthing attack, on–off attack, and selective behavior attack is depicted in Figure 2.3.

2.4   STATE-OF-THE-ART TRUST MANAGEMENT IN IOV

As a consequence of high dynamicity, vulnerable communications, and scarcity of pervasive intercommunication infrastructure, IoV is susceptible to attacks from both inside and outside the network. The dishonest vehicles counterfeit safety-critical data and often introduce transmission delays to disrupt vehicular services, consequently endangering the lives of drivers, passengers, and vulnerable pedestrians. During the past decade or so, a number of research studies in the literature have delineated on the notion of trust management for ensuring safe and reliable vehicular networks. This section depicts a comprehensive review of the literature on the trust management in vehicular networks categorized into six classes including: (1) conventional, (2) Bayesian inference-based, (3) blockchain-based, (4) deep/machine learning-based, (5) fuzzy logic-based, and (6) cryptography-based trust management models.

2.4.1   CONVENTIONAL TRUST MODELS

Conventional trust management models are defined as widely accepted frameworks that function without requiring complex data analysis or statistical inference tools. In this subsection, recent research employing conventional trust management models has been discussed in detail [47, 48, 49, 50, 51].

Ahmad et al. [47] presented MARINE that detects malicious vehicles, i.e., vehicles launching man-in-the-middle attacks, and cancel their credentials. MARINE is a hybrid trust model that also considers the possibility of an honest vehicle to initiate a false message due to malfunctioning hardware and a malicious vehicle to generate a genuine message. The proposed model takes into account the node trust, data trust, vehicle-to-vehicle trust, and the infrastructure-to-vehicle trust. Node trust is computed by aggregating the past interactions with the target vehicle and the opinions of its neighbors, whereas the data trust is calculated by taking into account the quality of the data received, neighbors' recommendations and the ability of the vehicle to forward messages. While computing the vehicle-to-vehicle trust, every vehicle forms a positive report that includes the honest vehicles and a negative report including details about the dishonest vehicles. These reports are then conveyed to the Roadside Unit (RSU) which, on its part, computes the infrastructure-to-vehicle trust and updates the above-mentioned reports. The up-to-date reports are then shared with the neighboring nodes. The proposed model has been tested against three attack scenarios utilizing simulation of urban mobility (SUMO) and vehicles in network simulation (VEINS).

Suo et al. [48] proposed a distributed, and a centralized trust-based system where trust authorities and vehicles join forces to alleviate dishonest behavior in vehicles. Every vehicle informs the trusted authority regarding suspicious behavior. The trusted authority, on the basis of suspicious activity information received from different nodes, decides if the certificate issued to a particular vehicle should be

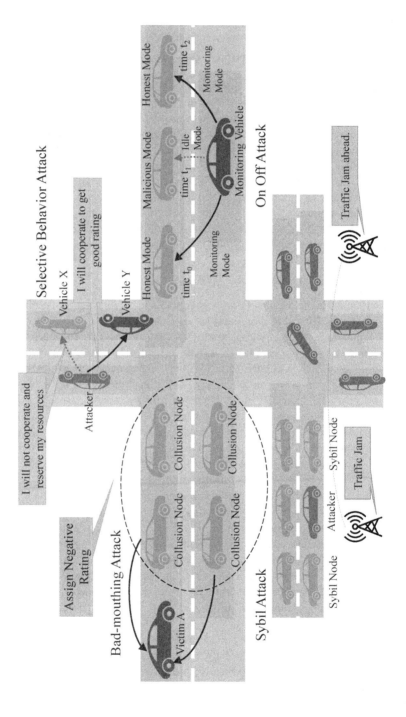

Figure 2.3 Attacks in the Internet of Vehicles. (Please note that the figure in the digital edition is displayed with color.)

revoked. The suggested system model addresses insider attacks and it is assumed that the adversary is capable of counterfeiting messages and disseminating them to the vehicles and roadside units in its vicinity via jeopardized vehicles. The trusted authority takes into account both the direct and the indirect interaction with the target vehicle. Different contributing parameters are assigned different context-based weightage while aggregating the trust score. The vehicles with higher trust scores have a higher impact on the trust establishment process. Both architectures, centralized and distributed, are evaluated using a python-based simulation for four different kinds of dishonest behaviors. The absence of a global perspective and the risk of over-trust are two of the main concerns regarding the distributed architecture mentioned by the authors.

Mahmood et al. [49] proposed a hybrid trust management model that amalgamates trust score and available resources of vehicles to compute a composite metric which is utilized to elect a cluster head and a proxy cluster head for a vehicular cluster. Available resources encompass the weighted sum of the measure of remaining power and bandwidth of a vehicle, whereas the trust score is an average of the direct and the indirect trust scores of a vehicle. Subsequently, vehicles with the highest and the second highest composite metric are elected as the cluster head and proxy cluster head, respectively, while the vehicles with a composite metric falling below a predefined threshold are classified as malicious vehicles. The performance evaluation of the proposed model has been carried out employing MATLAB.

Noorullah et al. [50] proposed a forwarding approach for critical information in vehicular social networks, wherein following the legitimacy verification of the emergency notification utilizing the information regarding the location and the social media of the source vehicle, significance of vehicles is computed to identify the vehicles most famous among their peers with the aim of rapid dissemination of the notification. The most well-connected vehicle is the one that shares interests, has common contacts, and is more similar in behavior to its peers. For computing a vehicle's reputation, its contribution in the network and the recommendations by its neighbors are taken into account, which is then utilized in calculating the trust value of that vehicle. The vehicles whose assigned trust values are close to the highest possible trust score are more likely to further improve their reputation and vice versa. Consequently, the dishonest vehicles will be isolated from the forwarding process. Accordingly, the emergency message is disseminated through the network, utilizing the vehicle to vehicle and infrastructure communication. Simulations of the proposed scheme are carried out using VANETMobiSim and the performance evaluation metrics included the transmission rate, the propagation latency, the number of messages disseminated, the duration for which the emergency message will circulate in the network, and the number of vehicles selected for critical message dissemination.

Chuprov et al. [51] proposed a scheme to mitigate traffic management issues on the crossroads by identifying the vehicles sending illegitimate messages, wherein three parameters, truth, reputation, and trust, each having a value within [0, 1], are computed to assess the legitimacy of the data sent by vehicles. Truth being the opinion regarding the legitimacy of the message exchanged by vehicles, reputation is defined as the temporal function of the truth value, and trust is the weighted aggregation of both of the above stated parameters. The computed trust score is compared with the predefined threshold and the vehicles having a trust score greater than the said threshold are considered trustworthy. The vehicle identified as the source of the misleading information, i.e., the untrustworthy vehicle, is isolated from interacting with its peer vehicles. The performance evaluation of the said system is conducted first by using a customized simulator and then the results are also validated utilizing hardware simulations based on an autonomous vehicle model developed by the authors.

2.4.2 BAYESIAN INFERENCE-BASED TRUST MODEL

Bayesian inference employs Bayesian theory that delineates uncertainty of data-centric modeling and inference relying on probability and statistics [52]. Bayesian statistics utilize prior distribution for probabilistic distribution of parameters which is amalgamated with the likelihood function to generate posterior distribution [53]. This subsection comprises detailed discussions on recent research in vehicular trust management models utilizing Bayesian inference [54, 55, 56, 57, 58]. Zhang et al. [54] proposed a TrustRank algorithm-based trust management model that takes into consideration both local and the global trust of the vehicles. The local trust is computed by applying the Bayesian inference model to the past interactions of the vehicles. Once the local trust values are computed, a trust link graph is constructed. In order to calculate the global trust, social parameters based on the driver (e.g., age, driving license score, driving age), the vehicle (e.g., vehicle type, handling stability, breaking performance), and the behavior (e.g., number of speeding tickets, number of traffic violations) are combined with the local trust values and the previous global trust values before applying the TrustRank based algorithm. The most trustworthy vehicles named as the seed vehicles are identified using the PageRank algorithm and these vehicles, subsequently, help in determining the trust values of other vehicles. Simulations are performed using VEINS and the evaluation of the proposed model is measured using two performance metrics, i.e., true negative and true positive rates. Three different attacks have been considered while evaluating the system model, i.e., newcomer attack, on–off attack, and collusion attack.

He et al. [55] envisaged a trust management scheme for enhancing the security of cognitive radio based VANETS and detected the JSSDT (i.e., joint spectrum sensing and data transmission) attackers that counterfeit reports and drop data in the spectrum sensing and transmission phases, respectively. While performing trust computations, an aggregation of weighted direct and indirect trust is calculated. The information regarding the neighboring vehicles' behavioral patterns is acquired, the neighbor trust is computed by employing techniques such as Bayesian inference, and is forwarded to other components of the model for other applications such as the data transmission unit which may utilize the computed trust score for route discovery, and the spectrum sensing unit which may utilize the calculated trust as a weightage for aggregation of spectrum detection. The performance of the proposed model is evaluated in terms of false alarm and miss detection probability, latency, and throughput.

Fang et al. [56] proposed a trust management model that employs Bayesian network to prevent on–off attack. The trust computations aggregate weighted direct and indirect trust, direct trust being the trust score relying on the direct interactions, both current and past, between two vehicles (i.e., a trustor and a trustee), whereas the indirect trust is the highest direct trust value assigned to the trustee by all of its neighboring vehicles, i.e., trustors. In the said attack, the vehicle alternates between honest and dishonest conduct quite frequently, consequently, the malicious vehicles end up achieving elevated trust scores. A window to identify the attack is defined based on the interactions between the trustor and the trustee. Every window has a highest, and a lowest trust score assigned to the trustee by the trustor and the number of times the trustee alters between the highest and the lowest score is counted. The dishonest vehicles switch from high to low and vice versa more often. Furthermore, their extreme trust scores are higher in comparison to honest vehicles which results in a smaller difference between the extremes and a higher switch count. If the switch count exceeds a predefined threshold, and the difference between the extremes is smaller or the highest trust score is greater than another predefined threshold, the vehicle is tagged as a malicious one. Simulations of the proposed model are carried out using MATLAB.

Li et al. [57] proposed a secure content delivery framework amalgamating the notions of trust and game theory. The vehicles are evaluated relying on their positivity and ability to communicate with their peers. Whenever a pair of vehicles communicate, the evaluator assigns an evaluation value to the evaluatee which is then cached in the evaluatee's local storage. An average of this evaluation value and a punishment value is combined to compute the trust value of the evaluatee. To minimize the effects of malicious activities, the vehicles are given the opportunity to challenge the punishment value assigned to them by their peers. Moreover, an evaluatee is evaluated by the same evaluator only once. On the other hand, RSUs are evaluated based on quality of service and reliability, and the average of this evaluation along with the punishment scores are combined to calculate the trust score for the target RSU.

Talal et al. [58] proposed a Bayesian inference-based decentralized trust model that takes into consideration the quality of direct interactions among the vehicles and the event related data transmitted by a vehicle. A belief function is defined to update the trust scores of a vehicle relying on the correlation among the event information that the target vehicle transmitted and the actual status of that particular event. The proposed method assigns a low initial trust score based on the punishing strategy to any vehicle new to the network to prevent dishonest vehicles from gaining advantage by leaving and joining the network frequently to gain high trust scores. To overcome the negative impacts of the said punishing strategy, i.e., the lack of collaboration opportunities available for the newcomer due to a low trust score, a trust-based vehicular coalition formation scheme to encourage collaboration among vehicles is utilized. The performance analysis of the proposed scheme is performed on MATLAB.

2.4.3 BLOCKCHAIN-BASED TRUST MODEL

Blockchain technology deals with the distributed digital ledger of transactions. It consists of unalterable decentralized database comprising blocks of data forming chains [59, 60]. In this subsection, a detailed overview of the recent research in trust management models employing blockchain technology has been presented [62, 63, 61, 64, 65]. Javaid et al. [62] proposed a privacy preserving model that utilizes blockchain for exchange of information as well as trust management in a distributed architecture. The vehicles are registered in the network which helps in developing information provenience and certificates are issued to them by a certificate authority (i.e., an RSU) to achieve data exchange security. To ensure the data trustworthiness, physical unclonable functions (PUF) are utilized after the registration of each vehicle. When data is generated, the list of trusted registered vehicles is examined for the originating vehicle. If the system is successful in locating the vehicle in the trusted list and the PUF response is also correct, a certificate is issued. The proposed model was simulated employing an Ethereum virtual machine and a threat model with an adversary that can imitate or impersonate a vehicle and transmit counterfeited information to the RSU and alter the information sent by a genuine vehicle is utilized for system evaluation.

Khan et al. [63] proposed a model that amalgamates blockchain and trust for misbehavior prevention, wherein a set of public and private keys is generated for every new vehicle, and a certificate is issued to the vehicle, which, in addition to the Certificate Blockchain (CertBC) having this certificate in its record and Revocation Blockchain (RevBC) not having the public key of the vehicle in its record, is used to authenticate the vehicle preceding the trust score acquisition from Trust Blockchain (TrustBC) and the information sharing among the vehicles. When an incident is reported by the vehicle, the receiving vehicle computes the legitimacy and the trust of the report, records it in a trust set, and employs it to calculate the likelihood of the reported incident happening. The report is considered legitimate if the resulting likelihood is greater than the predefined threshold and a positive ranking is assigned to it before it is recorded in the Message Blockchain (MesBC), which is forwarded to the RSU. The greater the number of positive rankings assigned to a vehicle, the more trustworthy the vehicle is, whereas a higher number of negative rankings (i.e., greater than a predefined threshold) results in the vehicle's public key and the certificate cancellation. The RSU, on the receipt of MesBC, computes the updated trust score of the vehicle and informs the network about it before recording it to the TrustBC. In order to become a miner, the hash value computed by the RSU should not exceed the predefined threshold and the sum of the absolute hash values of the RSU should not exceed the highest sum of these values. The block of the miner is then published into the blockchain and it is ensured that the blockchain of every RSU is identical. The performance evaluation of the proposed scheme is conducted by utilizing VEINS, SUMO, and OMNET++ (i.e., Objective Modular Network Testbed in C++), with and without introducing the denial of service attack.

Lu et al. [61] presented a trust management scheme that relies on the blockchain technology to ensure privacy preservation while the certification authority (CA) issues and revokes certificates. It is achieved by splitting the linkage among a vehicle's true identity and its public key. Any action taken by the CA is recorded evidently in the blockchain without exposing any sensitive details regarding vehicles to make sure a vehicle's public key could be utilized as its authenticated pseudonym. Furthermore, every vehicle is assessed relying on the legitimacy of the information disseminated by it in addition to the neighbors' opinion towards the said vehicle. The record of all the messages is maintained in the blockchain and is used as an evidence to compute the reputation score for each vehicle which helps alleviate dishonest behavior and dissemination of counterfeited messages. The vehicles are rewarded for their cooperation, honesty, and reporting misconduct, whereas the vehicles are liable to a penalty for misconduct and collusion. The performance of the proposed scheme is assessed in terms of overhead concerning the storage, transmission, and computation, however, the simulation platform has not been mentioned.

Yang et al. [64] proposed a blockchain based decentralized trust management model, wherein the vehicles evaluate the messages received from other vehicles and notify the RSUs about their evaluation results. The RSUs then compute the entity-based trust scores for the vehicles and create trust blocks. The RSU with the highest number of trust values in its block is selected as a miner to update the trust score of the particular vehicle by adding their block first. The adversarial model includes the spoofing attack where dishonest vehicles can counterfeit safety messages, and bad-mouthing attack where vehicles provide dishonest assessment on the legitimacy of messages. The employment of the notion of blockchain in the trust management process provides a decentralized architecture, prevention from data manipulation, persistent trust records throughout the network, fast convergence, and the information regarding the trust scores of a particular vehicle are easily available to all the RSUs. Simulations of the proposed scheme are carried out using vehicular and blockchain simulation platform on MATLAB.

Kang et al. [65] proposed a blockchain based trust model that selects evaluators called miners based on their trustworthiness in previous interactions. These miners are responsible for the creation, distribution, and validation of different blocks. Every node, while computing the reputation on a target RSU, incorporates the recommendations from all the other nodes utilizing subjective logic. Moreover, different influencing parameters, i.e., weights are introduced according to how often the two nodes interacted, how recent the latest interaction between the two was, and the outcome of the interaction, are taken into consideration. Subsequently, the weighted recommendations are aggregated to obtain a single recommendation prior to the accumulation of the direct and the recommended opinions. To encourage the participation of the verifiers in the block validation process, a reward is offered, and these verifiers, as per their reputation, are offered contracts by the block managers. Convex (CVX) tool based on MATLAB is utilized to optimize the reward process.

2.4.4 DEEP/MACHINE LEARNING-BASED TRUST MODEL

Machine learning is a subset of artificial intelligence and relies on learning from experience (i.e., data) to forecast and make decisions with precision over time [66].

Deep learning, a subgroup of machine learning, focuses on simulating the way a human brain works to learn from experience (i.e., large volume of data) by employing neural networks with multiple layers [67]. This subsection provides a detailed review of the recent research in trust management models applying the notion of machine learning and deep learning [69, 70, 68, 71, 72]. Tangade et al. [69] proposed a trust management model that utilizes the notion of deep learning to enhance the reliability and offers reduced latency. Each vehicle communicates with the neighboring vehicles and based on this communication, reward points are granted to the vehicles that are used to categorize the drivers/messages as honest or dishonest and, subsequently, utilized for trust score computation by employing deep neural network. A message generated by a vehicle is broadcasted and upon receipt at the RSU, the source is authenticated, and deep neural network is employed to compute the reward points taking the factors concerning the driver's behavior into consideration. The received message is classified as honest or dishonest utilizing a deep neural network by the RSU and, subsequently, the mediator trusted authority calculates the updated trust score of the particular vehicle. The proposed model is evaluated via simulations carried out on TensorFlow and Network Simulator (NS-3).

Zhang et al. [70] suggested a trust management model for software-defined networking based VANETs, wherein the route discovery is ascertained by evaluating the trustworthiness of the next hop neighbors. The said heuristic encompasses state, action, and reward, and contains information pertaining to the forwarding ratio matrix, next hop neighbor selection made by the SDN (software-defined network) controller, and the route trust evaluation, respectively. Furthermore, the authors' defined a minimum acceptable trust score and the vehicles possessing a trust score below the same are categorized as dishonest vehicles. When a vehicle originates a message and the data routing information is unknown, route discovery method and trust calculations are utilized to learn the best data forwarding information. As a vehicle's position and forwarding ratio are likely to change, the trust of that particular vehicle is inclined to change which, subsequently, affects the trustworthiness of the discovered path. Simulations are carried out on TensorFlow and OPNET.

Siddiqui et al. [68] presented a trust management model relying on machine learning to compute an optimal threshold and to identify malicious vehicles in a vehicular network utilizing three contributing parameters, i.e., similarity, familiarity, and packet delivery ratio. The proposed model employs multiple unsupervised learning algorithms to cluster the data for label assignment prior to applying diverse supervised learning algorithms to classify honest and dishonest vehicles, and to acquire an optimal threshold. Simulations for the proposed scheme are carried out on MATLAB.

Gyawali et al. [71] proposed a misbehavior detection scheme relying on hybrid collaborative machine learning and reputation where machine learning is employed to identify malicious messages, whereas reputation is utilized to evaluate the trustworthiness of a vehicle. Every message from a trustworthy vehicle is assessed prior to the report being sent to the local authority which amalgamates the reports employing Dempster–Shafer theory in addition to using the vehicle's reputation or trust value to compute the updated reputation. Subsequently, the reputation score is shared with the certificate authority and a revocation alert is broadcasted if the reputation value of the vehicle falls below the predefined threshold. The performance evaluation of the proposed scheme is carried out employing VEINS, SUMO, and OMNET++.

Zhang et al. [72] presented a trust management model that relies on deep reinforcement learning approach to enhance communication among connected vehicles. The said trust management scheme integrates a dueling networking architecture inside the SDN's logically centralized controller to ensure a reliable route is established for data forwarding employing a deep neural network. The route selection process is initiated by the vehicle that wishes to forward data to another vehicle and the trustworthiness of each vehicle, along the path, is evaluated to select the directly connected neighbor that is best suited, i.e., the most trustworthy, as the next hop in the route from the source to the destination vehicle. Simulations of the proposed scheme are carried out on TensorFlow and OPNET.

2.4.5   FUZZY LOGIC-BASED TRUST MODELS

Fuzzy logic focuses on representing the imprecision of human reasoning for decision making in an imprecise and uncertain environment [73]. In this subsection, trust management models employing fuzzy logic have been presented in detail [74, 75, 76, 77, 78]. Guleng et al. [74] presented a decentralized trust management framework that employs fuzzy logic to amalgamate a vehicle's direct experience and the recommendations of its peers towards a target vehicle in order to tag the unintended dishonest behavior of the said target vehicle. Furthermore, besides the direct trust, an indirect trust score is also computed towards the vehicles that do not have a direct connection to the trustor employing the notion of reinforcement learning. While evaluating the direct trust, the proportion of the messages relayed by the target vehicle, the ratio of legitimate messages forwarded by the target vehicle, and the fraction of the identified incidents that were reported by the target vehicle, were considered prior to employing fuzzy logic. The indirect trust score is computed by inquiring the opinions of neighboring vehicles on the target vehicle by employing Q-learning where the trust value is decremented on every hop along the path from the node expressing the opinion to the inquirer. Simulations of the presented model are carried out using NS-2.34.

Souissi et al. [75] proposed a model that amalgamates trust, in terms of the degree of similarity, and fuzzy logic to guarantee legitimate location information. The central authority validates the location information by cross checking the attributes of the reported lane and the reporting vehicle prior to storing it locally for future reference, e.g., optimum route selection and the status of road traffic, etc. To compute the similarity, three input parameters, i.e., time, speed, and energy, are used as inputs to the fuzzy system. The higher the resulting similarity index, the higher the trust of the reported location information. The shared location information is characterized as malicious if the resulting similarity index is less than the predefined threshold. Simulations of the suggested system are carried out using MATLAB and SUMO.

Kumar et al. [76] amalgamated the notions of fuzzy logic and trust to select the best path between two nodes and to identify blackhole attacks. The relationship of vehicles is estimated using trust computations, wherein the proportion of the successfully forwarded messages by the neighbor from the number of messages this neighbor is expected to forward, the ratio of the number of messages received through the neighbor but generated by other nodes to the total count of received messages, and the acknowledgment of the message receipt are aggregated. The neighbors are ranked as bad, unknown, and good according to the relationship and the trust scores. To select the best path, the neighbor ranked as good is the preferred option for the next hop node selection to forward the data. The vehicles having a bad association are the ones with lower trust scores and are suspected as blackhole attackers. Simulations of the proposed model are carried out using NS-2 and SUMO.

Tan et al. [77] proposed the reputation-based trust management model, wherein a credit account reflecting a node's behavior is associated with every node. The higher the credit score, the more the node is preferred, whereas if the credits of a node are depleted, the said node is eradicated from the network. The trust score of a node takes into consideration the node's reputation, opinion of the neighboring nodes, and historical interactions with other nodes in the network. Graph theory and fuzzy logic are amalgamated to compute the entity-based trust, to avoid the trust scores from increasing quickly while still allowing a swift decrease in trust scores decaying mechanism is employed. The proportion of the messages successfully delivered and the mean delay value are chosen to be the trust computation parameters, and fuzzy functions are defined for them to evaluate the trustworthiness of the routes. The trust score of a route drops down if a dishonest vehicle exists in that route, therefore, this trust score can be utilized to compute a vehicle's trust score. Simulations of the proposed scheme are carried out on MoSim based on MATLAB.

Marmol et al. [78] amalgamated the notions of trust and reputation, wherein to accept or reject a message generated by vehicles, each vehicle computes the trust scores of its peers by employing fuzzy sets. While calculating the said trust values, the node's past reputation and the opinions of the roadside infrastructure and the other vehicles in the cluster are taken into consideration. Moreover, the vehicles are rewarded or punished as per the comparison of the final decision of their opinions regarding a particular message. If the source vehicle is proved to be dishonest, a notification is sent to the infrastructure and the information on the vehicle is added to the dishonest vehicle database if the number of negative opinions exceed a predefined threshold. Every message generated in the network has a severity level associated with it, accordingly, the message with a high severity level is considered trustworthy only if it is generated by a trustworthy vehicle. Simulations of the proposed model are carried out using trust and reputation model simulator (TRMSim-V2V) developed by the authors.

2.4.6   CRYPTOGRAPHY-BASED TRUST MODEL

Cryptography focuses on ciphering data to ensure confidentiality and to prevent unauthorized entities from interpreting the information [79]. This subsection discusses, in detail, the recent research employing the notion of trust along with cryptography [80, 81, 82, 83, 84]. Muhlbauer et al. [80] proposed a trust management model, wherein the notion of digital certificates and reputation are amalgamated in a centralized vehicular architecture without the necessity of constant connectivity with the road infrastructure. The proposed scheme relies on public key infrastructure (PKI) for vehicles where an ID, a set of public and private keys, and a certificate is assigned to each vehicle and RSU to be able to communicate and authenticate the exchanged messages. The incidents are validated by the traffic control authority (CCO) in a centralized manner. Every vehicle is required to have a frequent contact with a certificate authority that issues the certificates and pseudonyms to preserve privacy. A score is maintained by each vehicle regarding its own certified reputation which is utilized to compute trust among vehicles. Whenever a vehicle notifies its peers regarding an incident, the recipients verify the digital signatures of the source vehicle using the certificate issued to it prior to the evaluation of the message legitimacy. The proposed scheme employs reputation for weighted voting, and message selection by applying simple summation, and Bayesian inference-based reputation prior to the comparison of the resulting score with the predefined threshold. Simulations of the said model are carried out utilizing VEINS, SUMO, OMNET++, and MiXiM (i.e., a mixed simulator for wireless mobile communication network).

Gai et al. [81] proposed a trust management model, wherein cookies are used by an inquirer to rate, in the range [0, 1], the services provided by another vehicle which are then signed by a certificate authority to keep the vehicle from counterfeiting them. Whenever a vehicle entertains a request by another vehicle, it forwards its cookies along with the service requested which is used by the requester to evaluate the trustworthiness of the service provider. In the event of first interaction between the two, the trust score assigned by the requester is the same as the cookie reported by the service provider. However, if the two have interacted in the past, the requester computes an aggregate of weighted direct and indirect trust based on the cookies. The direct trust being the one computed by the cookies in the record of the requester based on their historic interactions, whereas the indirect trust is the one computed using the cookies shared by the service provider. Simulations of the proposed model are carried out on VANETsim.

Wang et al. [82] proposed an authentication framework that utilizes trust to expedite the re-authentication process in the event of handover between the former and the current RSU where vehicles dissociate from the previous RSU and connect to another RSU in their vicinity. The cloud server is responsible for the evaluation of the trust score of every vehicle based on its characteristics. The RSU utilizes the trust score of a vehicle to complete the authentication process and the creation of the session key. As a vehicle traverses from the service range of one RSU (i.e., former) to the other (i.e., current), a certificate affirming the handover is received by the vehicle, and the current RSU forwarded by the former RSU. A token is generated to the vehicle by the current RSU prior to the generation of the session key between the two. Simulations of the proposed scheme are carried out utilizing GNU MultiPrecision (GMP) and Pairing-based Cryptography (PBC) libraries, C language, and a Ubuntu based system.

Tangade et al. [83] proposed a trust management model relying on hybrid cryptography for authentication to ensure robust and efficient trust management. The trusted authority registers the vehicles, road side units, and intermediary trusted authorities prior to their participation in the network. The trustworthiness of these vehicles is then verified by its neighbors via exchange of a test message and the resulting trust score is forwarded to the trusted authority which is responsible for computing and updating the trust value of the target vehicle. When communicating with one another in the network, vehicles also send their trust score in addition to other information such as safety messages, and is verified by the receiving vehicle through comparison with the one stored at the trusted authority. The safety alerts are trusted if the compared trust scores are identical and greater than the predefined threshold else, they are discarded. The performance evaluation of the proposed scheme is carried out utilizing NS-3, SUMO, and MOVE (i.e., a mobility model generator).

Zhang et al. [84] presented a trust management scheme to prevent the election of malicious platoon heads and to preserve the privacy of participating vehicles utilizing paillier cryptosystem. A proof of handshake among a platoon head and the vehicle is generated by every vehicle joining a platoon. At the end of the journey, both the platoon head and the vehicle create and send driving reports to the RSU which, after verifying the vehicle's authenticity, computes the reputation of the platoon head based on the vehicle's trust score and opinion before delivering it to the service provider. Subsequently, the service provider assesses the performance of the vehicle prior to forwarding it to the trusted authority that forecasts the future behavior of the vehicle relying on the past experiences. The performance evaluation of the platoon selection is carried out by utilizing a Java-based simulation, whereas the network performance is assessed by employing NS-2 and SUMO.

2.5   RESEARCH CHALLENGES

A thorough glimpse of the existing literature demonstrates a considerable amount of research in vehicular trust management models. Nevertheless, they do not account for the challenges as follows.

2.5.1   COLD START

Owing to the high mobility, cold start or bootstrapping is a crucial problem in vehicular trust management models. No information is available regarding the previous interactions for newly joining vehicles which makes it impossible to compute the trust score relying on the historical interactions for a newcomer. Consequently, a static initial trust value is assigned to all incoming vehicles. If the said initial value is kept too low, there is a high chance that an honest vehicle will get eliminated from the network owing to a low trust score. On the contrary, if it is set too high, it will take too long to eradicate dishonest nodes (based on trust scores), consequently, jeopardizing the network security. The bootstrapping issue has been addressed in social networks and recommender systems, nevertheless, it is still a major challenge in vehicular trust management models [85, 86].

2.5.2   DATA SCARCITY

Due to the highly dynamic topology of vehicular networks, scarcity of information availability can lead to ineffective trust management and failure to identify misbehaving entities. Analogous to the cold start problem, data scarcity is caused by minimal or no prior interactions by a vehicle in the network. In the case of a newcomer vehicle, there are no historical interactions, whereas in a low traffic density scenario, there is a limited number of interactions available. Accurate trust computations and vehicle eviction relying on these computations require sufficient information regarding a vehicle's past experiences with its peers. Amalgamating both direct and indirect observations regarding a target vehicle occasionally helps with data scarcity; however, trust management models relying primarily on entity-based trust do not perform well in sparse environments [87].

2.5.3   STEADY THRESHOLD

While designing trust management models, a steady predefined threshold is often employed to detect malicious vehicles, i.e., the vehicles having a greater trust score than the said threshold are classified as trustworthy, whereas the vehicles with trust values falling below the same threshold are categorized as malicious. As mentioned earlier in Section 2.3.5, intelligent attackers (i.e., on–off attackers) do not depict malicious behavior persistently, i.e., they switch their behaviors from honest to dishonest and back frequently in order to avoid detection. Therefore, a steady threshold does not help in the elimination of these intelligent attackers. To mitigate on-off attacks, adaptive threshold is employed which also helps in early detection of dishonest vehicles; however, trust management models with such a threshold are quite computer intensive [5].

2.5.4   THRESHOLD QUANTIFICATION

With the intention to identify misbehaving entities in a vehicular network, an acceptable trust threshold is often employed, i.e., vehicles with a lower trust value as compared to the said threshold are tagged as untrustworthy, whereas the ones with a higher trust score are grouped as trustworthy. It is, therefore, of paramount importance that the value of such threshold is precisely defined so as to detect and evict malicious vehicles accurately from the network. If the said threshold is kept too high, the probability of honest vehicles getting eliminated increases. If the threshold is set too low, the malicious vehicles will stay in the network for too long, consequently, causing harm to the network. The existing literature assigns a steady value as a threshold without taking the dynamic nature of the vehicular network into consideration [26].

2.5.5   WEIGHTS QUANTIFICATION

The trust computation process requires the contributing trust parameters (e.g., direct and indirect trust) to be aggregated to acquire a final trust score for a trustee.

In some cases, the contributing parameters are averaged out to obtain the final trust score which implies that each contributing factor has the exact same impact on the final trust score. Alternatively, the notion of weights is commonly applied, wherein different contributing parameters are assigned different weightage relying on their respective contribution/importance in the final trust value computation. Determining precise values for these weights in proportion to the relevance and significance of the said parameters is of great importance. The existing research literature addresses the quantification of the aforementioned weights to some extent, nevertheless, this problem demands considerable attention [68].

In accordance with the aforementioned research challenges, this book delineates solutions to the issues related to steady threshold, threshold quantification, and weight quantification, along with the introduction of context awareness (Chapter 3), time awareness (Chapter 4), machine learning (Chapter 5), and a variety of trust parameters to achieve diverse results.

2.6   CHAPTER SUMMARY

To satisfy the ever-growing transportation demands in megacities, efficient and effective utilization of the existing transportation infrastructure is of paramount importance, especially in ITS in the context of smart cities. Smart connected vehicles form IoV network that facilitates both non-safety, e.g., infotainment, and safety-critical, e.g., warning and alert generating applications, by exploiting V2X communications. To ascertain the reliability and trustworthiness of such communications, the notion of trust is introduced and, subsequently, trust management schemes are employed in vehicular networks. This chapter presents a comprehensive review of the state-of-the-art trust management models in the IoV employing diverse computational domains. The chapter emphasizes comparing the said trust management schemes with respect to the evaluation tools utilized, the quantification of weights applied during trust aggregation, misbehavior detection, attack resistance, and the quantification of the threshold defined for misbehavior detection. Furthermore, a brief glimpse of the IoV layered architecture, the notion of trust and its constituents, and the attacks associated with vehicular networks is also provided. Finally, open research directions in the area are discussed as well. In a nutshell, this review can provide useful guidance for future research in trust management in the IoV.

As discussed in open directions (Section 2.5), weights and threshold quantification are vital to accumulating a precise yet dynamic trust management model. It is extremely important to take account of the network, the context as well as the communication parameters while designing such a framework to ensure the influence of the devised threshold and that of weights is not only adaptive but is also rational. Moreover, it is also critical to introduce attack resistance when formulating individual trust attributes, e.g., against on-off attacks or selective node attack. Accordingly, the next chapter will emphasize on developing a trust management framework relying on the context information related to the interaction among a pair of vehicles, logical and dynamic trust attributes and their corresponding (quantified) weights, and quantification of an adaptive threshold to cater for the dynamic nature of vehicle networks for misbehavior detection.

REFERENCES

1. C. A. Kerrache, C. T. Calafate, J.-C. Cano, N. Lagraa, and P. Manzoni. *Trust Management for Vehicular Networks: An Adversary-oriented Overview.* IEEE Access 4, 9293 (2016).

2. Z. Lu, G. Qu, and Z. Liu. *A Survey on Recent Advances in Vehicular Network Security, Trust, and Privacy.* IEEE Transactions on Intelligent Transportation Systems 20(2), 760 (2018).

3. R. Hussain, J. Lee, and S. Zeadally. *Trust in VANET: A Survey of Current Solutions and Future Research Opportunities.* IEEE Transactions on Intelligent Transportation Systems 22(5), 2553 (2020).

4. S. A. Siddiqui, A. Mahmood, Q. Z. Sheng, H. Suzuki, and W. Ni. *A Survey of Trust Management in the Internet of Vehicles.* Electronics 10(18), 2223 (2021).

5. A. Mahmood, W. E. Zhang, Q. Z. Sheng, S. A. Siddiqui, and A. Aljubairy. *Trust Management for Software-defined Heterogeneous Vehicular Ad Hoc Networks.* In *Security, Privacy and Trust in the IoT Environment*, pp. 203–226 (Springer, 2019).

6. K. Alshouiliy and D. P. Agrawal. *Confluence of 4G LTE, 5G, Fog, and Cloud Computing and Understanding Security Issues.* In *Fog/Edge Computing for Security, Privacy, and Applications*, pp. 3–32 (Springer, 2021).

7. J. K. Burgoon, N. E. Dunbar, and M. L. Jensen. *An Integrated Spiral Model of Trust.* In *Detecting Trust and Deception in Group Interaction,* pp. 11–33 (Springer, 2021).

8. S. M. Ghafari, A. Beheshti, A. Joshi, C. Paris, A. Mahmood, S. Yakhchi, and M. A. Orgun. *A Survey on Trust Prediction in Online Social Networks.* IEEE Access 8, 144292 (2020).

9. A. Ben-Ner and F. Halldorsson. *Trusting and Trustworthiness: What are They, How to Measure Them, and What Affects Them.* Journal of Economic Psychology 31(1), 64 (2010).

10. A. Jøsang, R. Ismail, and C. Boyd. *A Survey of Trust and Reputation Systems for Online Service Provision.* Decision Support Systems 43(2), 618 (2007).

11. P. Håkansson and H. Witmer. *Social Media and Trust: A Systematic Literature Review.* Journal of Business and Economics 6(3), 517 (2015).

12. S. Ba and P. A. Pavlou. *Evidence of the Effect of Trust Building Technology in Electronic Markets: Price Premiums and Buyer Behavior.* MIS quarterly pp. 243–268 (2002).

13. N. B. Truong, T.-W. Um, B. Zhou, and G. M. Lee. *From Personal Experience to Global Reputation for Trust Evaluation in the Social Internet of Things.* In *2017 IEEE Global Communications Conference (GLOBECOM)*, pp. 1–7 (IEEE, 2017).

14. S. A. Soleymani, A. H. Abdullah, W. H. Hassan, M. H. Anisi, S. Goudarzi, M. A. Rezazadeh Baee, and S. Mandala. *Trust Management in Vehicular Ad Hoc Network: A Systematic Review.* EURASIP Journal on Wireless Communications and Networking 2015(1), 1 (2015).

15. Q. Cui, Z. Zhu, W. Ni, X. Tao, and P. Zhang. *Edge-Intelligence-Empowered, Unified Authentication and Trust Evaluation for Heterogeneous Beyond 5G Systems.* IEEE Wireless Communications 28(2), 78 (2021).

16. W. Yong-hao. *A Trust Management Model for Internet of Vehicles.* In *Proceedings of the 2020 4th International Conference on Cryptography, Security and Privacy*, pp. 136–140 (2020).

17. U. Jayasinghe, A. Otebolaku, T.-W. Um, and G. M. Lee. *Data-centric Trust Evaluation and Prediction Framework for IOT*. In *2017 ITU Kaleidoscope: Challenges for a Data-Driven Society (ITU K)*, pp. 1–7 (2017).

18. N. Yang. *A Similarity based Trust and Reputation Management Framework for VANETs*. International Journal of Future Generation Communication and Networking 6(2), 25 (2013).

19. R. S. D. Sousa, A. Boukerche, and A. A. F. Loureiro. *Vehicle Trajectory Similarity: Models, Methods, and Applications* 53(5) (2020).

20. A. Mahmood, S. A. Siddiqui, W. E. Zhang, and Q. Z. Sheng. *A Hybrid Trust Management Model for Secure and Resource Efficient Vehicular Ad Hoc Networks*. In *2019 20th International Conference on Parallel and Distributed Computing, Applications and Technologies (PDCAT)*, pp. 154–159 (2019).

21. H. Xia, F. Xiao, S.-s. Zhang, C.-q. Hu, and X.-Z. Cheng. *Trustworthiness Inference Framework in the Social Internet of Things: A Context-Aware Approach*. In *IEEE INFOCOM 2019 - IEEE Conference on Computer Communications*, pp. 838–846 (2019).

22. X. Huang, R. Yu, J. Kang, and Y. Zhang. *Distributed Reputation Management for Secure and Efficient Vehicular Edge Computing and Networks*. IEEE Access 5, 25408 (2017).

23. D. Wang, X. Chen, H. Wu, R. Yu, and Y. Zhao. *A Blockchain-Based Vehicle-Trust Management Framework Under a Crowdsourcing Environment*. In *2020 IEEE 19th International Conference on Trust, Security and Privacy in Computing and Communications (TrustCom)*, pp. 1950–1955 (2020).

24. Y. Yu, Z. Jia, W. Tao, B. Xue, and C. Lee. *An Efficient Trust Evaluation Scheme for Node Behavior Detection in the Internet of Things*. Wireless Personal Communications 93(2), 571 (2017).

25. J. Lim, D. Keum, and Y.-B. Ko. *A Stepwise and Hybrid Trust Evaluation Scheme for Tactical Wireless Sensor Networks*. Sensors 20(4) (2020).

26. U. Jayasinghe, G. M. Lee, T.-W. Um, and Q. Shi. *Machine Learning Based Trust Computational Model for IoT Services*. IEEE Transactions on Sustainable Computing 4(1), 39 (2019).

27. G.-U. Rehman, A. Ghani, M. Zubair, S. H. A. Naqvi, D. Singh, and S. Muhammad. *IPS: Incentive and Punishment Scheme for Omitting Selfishness in the Internet of Vehicles (IoV)*. IEEE Access 7, 109026 (2019).

28. N. Haddadou, A. Rachedi, and Y. Ghamri-Doudane. *A Job Market Signaling Scheme for Incentive and Trust Management in Vehicular Ad Hoc Networks*. IEEE Transactions on Vehicular Technology 64(8), 3657 (2015).

29. J. Zhang. *A Survey on Trust Management for VANETs*. In *2011 IEEE International Conference on Advanced Information Networking and Applications*, pp. 105–112 (2011).

30. M. Raya, P. Papadimitratos, V. D. Gligor, and J.-P. Hubaux. *On Data-Centric Trust Establishment in Ephemeral Ad Hoc Networks*. In *IEEE INFOCOM 2008 - The 27th Conference on Computer Communications*, pp. 1238–1246 (2008).

31. S. Gurung, D. Lin, A. Squicciarini, and E. Bertino. *Information-oriented Trustworthiness Evaluation in Vehicular Ad-hoc Networks*. In J. Lopez, X. Huang, and R. Sandhu, eds., *Network and System Security*, pp. 94–108 (Springer Berlin Heidelberg, Berlin, Heidelberg, 2013).

32. R. Sugumar, A. Rengarajan, and C. Jayakumar. *Trust based Authentication Technique for Cluster based Vehicular Ad Hoc Networks (VANET)*. Wireless Networks 24(2), 373 (2018).

33. H. Hasrouny, A. E. Samhat, C. Bassil, and A. Laouiti. *A Security Solution for V2V Communication within VANETs*. In 2018 Wireless Days (WD), pp. 181–183 (2018).

34. S. Dahmane, C. A. Kerrache, N. Lagraa, and P. Lorenz. *WeiSTARS: A Weighted Trust-aware Relay Selection Scheme for VANET*. In *2017 IEEE International Conference on Communications (ICC)*, pp. 1–6 (2017).

35. F. Ahmad, F. Kurugollu, C. A. Kerrache, S. Sezer, and L. Liu. *NOTRINO: A NOvel Hybrid Trust Management Scheme for Internet-of-Vehicles*. IEEE Transactions on Vehicular Technology 70(9), 9244 (2021).

36. S. Oubabas, R. Aoudjit, J. J. P. C. Rodrigues, and S. Talbi. *Secure and Stable Vehicular Ad Hoc Network Clustering Algorithm based on Hybrid Mobility Similarities and Trust Management Scheme*. Vehicular Communications 13, 128 (2018).

37. G. Gür, Serif Bahtiyar, and F. Alagöz. *Chapter 30 - Security Analysis of Computer Networks: Key Concepts and Methodologies*. In M. S. Obaidat, P. Nicopolitidis, and F. Zarai, eds., *Modeling and Simulation of Computer Networks and Systems*, pp. 861–898 (Morgan Kaufmann, Boston, 2015).

38. S. Kim. *Chapter 2 - Blockchain for a Trust Network Among Intelligent Vehicles*. In P. Raj and G. C. Deka, eds., *Blockchain Technology: Platforms, Tools and Use Cases*, vol. 111 of Advances in Computers, pp. 43–68 (Elsevier, 2018).

39. S. S. Tangade and S. S. Manvi. *A Survey on Attacks, Security and Trust Management Solutions in VANETs*. In *2013 Fourth International Conference on Computing, Communications and Networking Technologies (ICCCNT)*, pp. 1–6 (2013).

40. P. Patel and R. Jhaveri. *A Honeypot Scheme to Detect Selfish Vehicles in Vehicular Ad-hoc Network*. In H. . Vishwakarma and S. Akashe, eds., *Computing and Network Sustainability*, pp. 389–401 (Springer Singapore, Singapore, 2017).

41. F. Ahmad, A. Adnane, V. N. Franqueira, F. Kurugollu, and L. Liu. *Man-in-the-middle Attacks in Vehicular Ad-hoc Networks: Evaluating the Impact of Attackers' Strategies*. Sensors 18(11), 4040 (2018).

42. S. Hamdan, A. Hudaib, and A. Awajan. *Detecting Sybil Attacks in Vehicular Ad Hoc Networks*. International Journal of Parallel, Emergent and Distributed Systems 36(2), 69 (2021).

43. Z. Bankovic, J. C. Vallejo, D. Fraga, and J. M. Moya. *Detecting Bad-Mouthing Attacks on Reputation Systems Using Self-Organizing Maps*. In Á. Herrero and E. Corchado, eds., *Computational Intelligence in Security for Information Systems*, pp. 9–16 (Springer Berlin Heidelberg, Berlin, Heidelberg, 2011).

44. J. Wang, Y. Zhang, Y. Wang, and X. Gu. *RPRep: A Robust and Privacy-preserving Reputation Management Scheme for Pseudonym-Enabled VANETs*. International Journal of Distributed Sensor Networks 12(3), 6138251 (2016).

45. J.-M. Chen, T.-T. Li, and J. Panneerselvam. *TMEC: A Trust Management based on Evidence Combinationon Attack-resistant and Collaborative Internet of Vehicles*. IEEE Access 7, 148913 (2019).

46. P. S. Gautham and R. Shanmughasundaram. *Detection and Isolation of Black Hole in VANET*. In *2017 International Conference on Intelligent Computing, Instrumentation and Control Technologies (ICICICT)*, pp. 1534–1539 (IEEE, 2017).

47. F. Ahmad, F. Kurugollu, A. Adnane, R. Hussain, and F. Hussain. *MARINE: Man-in-the-Middle Attack Resistant Trust Model in Connected Vehicles*. IEEE Internet of Things Journal 7(4), 3310 (2020).

48. D. Suo and S. E. Sarma. *Real-time Trust-Building Schemes for Mitigating Malicious Behaviors in Connected and Automated Vehicles*. In *2019 IEEE Intelligent Transportation Systems Conference (ITSC)*, pp. 1142–1149 (2019).

49. A. Mahmood, B. Butler, W. E. Zhang, Q. Z. Sheng, and S. A. Siddiqui. *A Hybrid Trust Management Heuristic for VANETs*. In *2019 IEEE International Conference on Pervasive Computing and Communications Workshops (PerCom Workshops)*, pp. 748–752 (2019).

50. N. Ullah, X. Kong, Z. Ning, A. Tolba, M. Alrashoud, and F. Xia. *Emergency Warning Messages Dissemination in Vehicular Social Networks: A Trust based Scheme*. Vehicular Communications 22, 100199 (2020).

51. S. Chuprov, I. Viksnin, I. Kim, E. Marinenkov, M. Usova, E. Lazarev, T. Melnikov, and D. Zakoldaev. *Reputation and Trust Approach for Security and Safety Assurance in Intersection Management System*. Energies 12(23) (2019).

52. Z. Fei, K. Liu, B. Huang, Y. Zheng, and X. Xiang. *Dirichlet Process Mixture Model Based Nonparametric Bayesian Modeling and Variational Inference*. In *2019 Chinese Automation Congress (CAC)*, pp. 3048–3051 (2019).

53. S. Jun. *Bayesian Inference and Learning for Neural Networks and Deep Learning*. In *2020 International Conference on Artificial Intelligence in Information and Communication (ICAIIC)*, pp. 569–571 (2020).

54. J. Zhang, K. Zheng, D. Zhang, and B. Yan. *AATMS: An Anti-Attack Trust Management Scheme in VANET*. IEEE Access 8, 21077 (2020).

55. Y. He, F. R. Yu, Z. Wei, and V. Leung. *Trust Management for Secure Cognitive Radio Vehicular Ad Hoc Networks*. Ad Hoc Networks 86, 154 (2019).

56. W. Fang, W. Zhang, Y. Liu, W. Yang, and Z. Gao. *BTDS: Bayesian-based Trust Decision Scheme for intelligent Connected Vehicles in VANETs*. Transactions on Emerging Telecommunications Technologies 31(12), e3879 (2020).

57. J. Li, R. Xing, Z. Su, N. Zhang, Y. Hui, T. H. Luan, and H. Shan. *Trust Based Secure Content Delivery in Vehicular Networks: A Bargaining Game Theoretical Approach*. IEEE Transactions on Vehicular Technology 69(3), 3267 (2020).

58. T. Halabi and M. Zulkernine. *Trust-based Cooperative Game Model for Secure Collaboration in the Internet of Vehicles*. In *ICC 2019 - 2019 IEEE International Conference on Communications (ICC)*, pp. 1–6 (2019).

59. M. Jayaprasanna, V. Soundharya, M. Suhana, and S. Sujatha. *A Block Chain based Management System for Detecting Counterfeit Product in Supply Chain*. In *2021 Third International Conference on Intelligent Communication Technologies and Virtual Mobile Networks (ICICV)*, pp. 253–257 (2021).

60. Z. Mahmood and J. Vacius. *Privacy-preserving Block-chain Framework Based on Ring Signatures (RSs) and Zero-Knowledge Proofs (ZKPs)*. In *2020 International Conference on Innovation and Intelligence for Informatics, Computing and Technologies (3ICT)*, pp. 1–6 (2020).

61. Z. Lu, Q. Wang, G. Qu, and Z. Liu. *BARS: A Blockchain-based Anonymous Reputation System for Trust Management in VANETs*. In *2018 17th IEEE International Conference on Trust, Security And Privacy in Computing and Communications/12th IEEE International Conference on Big Data Science and Engineering (TrustCom/BigDataSE)*, pp. 98–103 (IEEE, 2018).

62. U. Javaid, M. N. Aman, and B. Sikdar. *DrivMan: Driving Trust Management and Data Sharing in VANETs with Blockchain and Smart Contracts.* In *2019 IEEE 89th Vehicular Technology Conference (VTC2019-Spring)*, pp. 1–5 (2019).

63. A. S. Khan, K. Balan, Y. Javed, S. Tarmizi, and J. Abdullah. *Secure Trust-Based Blockchain Architecture to Prevent Attacks in VANET.* Sensors 19(22) (2019).

64. Z. Yang, K. Yang, L. Lei, K. Zheng, and V. C. M. Leung. *Blockchain-Based Decentralized Trust Management in Vehicular Networks.* IEEE Internet of Things Journal 6(2), 1495 (2019).

65. J. Kang, Z. Xiong, D. Niyato, D. Ye, D. I. Kim, and J. Zhao. *Toward Secure Blockchain-Enabled Internet of Vehicles: Optimizing Consensus Management Using Reputation and Contract Theory.* IEEE Transactions on Vehicular Technology 68(3), 2906 (2019).

66. S. Ray. *A Quick Review of Machine Learning Algorithms.* In *2019 International Conference on Machine Learning, Big Data, Cloud and Parallel Computing (COMITCon)*, pp. 35–39 (2019).

67. *What is Deep Learning?* https://machineLearningmastery.com/what-is-Deep-Learning/. Accessed: 2022-03-24.

68. S. A. Siddiqui, A. Mahmood, W. E. Zhang, and Q. Z. Sheng. *Machine Learning Based Trust Model for Misbehaviour Detection in Internet-of-Vehicles.* In T. Gedeon, K. W. Wong, and M. Lee, eds., *Neural Information Processing*, pp. 512–520 (Springer International Publishing, Cham, 2019).

69. S. Tangade, S. S. Manvi, and S. Hassan. *A Deep Learning based Driver Classification and Trust Computation in VANETs.* In *2019 IEEE 90th Vehicular Technology Conference (VTC2019-Fall)*, pp. 1–6 (2019).

70. D. Zhang, F. R. Yu, and R. Yang. *A Machine Learning Approach for Software-Defined Vehicular Ad Hoc Networks with Trust Management.* In *2018 IEEE Global Communications Conference (GLOBECOM)*, pp. 1–6 (2018).

71. S. Gyawali, Y. Qian, and R. Q. Hu. *Machine Learning and Reputation based Misbehavior Detection in Vehicular Communication Networks.* IEEE Transactions on Vehicular Technology 69(8), 8871 (2020).

72. D. Zhang, F. R. Yu, R. Yang, and H. Tang. *A Deep Reinforcement Learning-based Trust Management Scheme for Software-defined Vehicular Networks.* In *Proceedings of the 8th ACM Symposium on Design and Analysis of Intelligent Vehicular Networks and Applications*, pp. 1–7 (2018).

73. L. Zadeh. *Fuzzy Logic.* Computer 21(4), 83 (1988).

74. S. Guleng, C. Wu, X. Chen, X. Wang, T. Yoshinaga, and Y. Ji. *Decentralized Trust Evaluation in Vehicular Internet of Things.* IEEE Access 7, 15980 (2019).

75. I. Souissi, N. B. Azzouna, T. Berradia, and L. B. Said. *A New Fuzzy Logic based Model for Location Trust Estimation in Electric Vehicular Networks.* In L. Barolli, M. Takizawa, F. Xhafa, and T. Enokido, eds., *Advanced Information Networking and Applications*, pp. 341–352 (Springer International Publishing, Cham, 2020).

76. A. Kumar, P. Dadheech, M. K. Beniwal, B. Agarwal, and P. K. Patidar. *A Fuzzy Logic-based Control System for Detection and Mitigation of Blackhole Attack in Vehicular Ad Hoc Network.* In A. Chaudhary, C. Choudhary, M. K. Gupta, C. Lal, and T. Badal, eds., *Microservices in Big Data Analytics*, pp. 163–178 (Springer Singapore, Singapore, 2020).

77. S. Tan, X. Li, and Q. Dong. *A Trust Management System for Securing Data Plane of Ad-hoc Networks.* IEEE Transactions on Vehicular Technology 65(9), 7579 (2016).

78. F. Gómez Mármol and G. Martínez Pérez. *TRIP, A Trust and Reputation Infrastructure-based Proposal for Vehicular Ad Hoc Networks*. Journal of Network and Computer Applications 35(3), 934 (2012). Special Issue on Trusted Computing and Communications.

79. A. M. Qadir and N. Varol. *A Review Paper on Cryptography*. In *2019 7th International Symposium on Digital Forensics and Security (ISDFS)*, pp. 1–6 (2019).

80. R. Mühlbauer and J. H. Kleinschmidt. *Bring Your Own Reputation: A Feasible Trust System for Vehicular Ad Hoc Networks*. Journal of Sensor and Actuator Networks 7(3) (2018).

81. F. Gai, J. Zhang, P. Zhu, and X. Jiang. *Ratee-based Trust Management System for Internet of Vehicles*. In L. Ma, A. Khreishah, Y. Zhang, and M. Yan, eds., *Wireless Algorithms, Systems, and Applications*, pp. 344–355 (Springer International Publishing, Cham, 2017).

82. C. Wang, J. Shen, J.-F. Lai, and J. Liu. *A Trustworthiness-based Time-Efficient V2I Authentication Scheme for VANETs*. In Z. Zheng, H.-N. Dai, M. Tang, and X. Chen, eds., *Blockchain and Trustworthy Systems*, pp. 794–799 (Springer Singapore, Singapore, 2020).

83. S. Tangade, S. S. Manvi, and P. Lorenz. *Trust Management Scheme based on Hybrid Cryptography for Secure Communications in VANETs*. IEEE Transactions on Vehicular Technology 69(5), 5232 (2020).

84. C. Zhang, L. Zhu, C. Xu, K. Sharif, K. Ding, X. Liu, X. Du, and M. Guizani. *TPPR: A Trust-based and Privacy-preserving Platoon Recommendation Scheme in VANET*. IEEE Transactions on Services Computing pp. 1–1 (2019).

85. D. Alishev, R. Hussain, W. Nawaz, and J. Lee. *Social-aware Bootstrapping and Trust Establishing Mechanism for Vehicular Social Networks*. In *2017 IEEE 85th Vehicular Technology Conference (VTC Spring)*, pp. 1–5 (2017).

86. L. H. Son. *Dealing with the New User Cold-start Problem in Recommender Systems: A Comparative Review*. Information Systems 58, 87 (2016).

87. F. Ahmad, J. Hall, A. Adnane, and V. N. L. Franqueira. *Faith in Vehicles: A Set of Evaluation Criteria for Trust Management in Vehicular Ad-hoc Network*. In *2017 IEEE International Conference on Internet of Things (iThings) and IEEE Green Computing and Communications (GreenCom) and IEEE Cyber, Physical and Social Computing (CPSCom) and IEEE Smart Data (SmartData)*, pp. 44–52 (2017).

3 Context-aware Trust Management for the Internet of Vehicles

This chapter primarily emphasizes on the quantification of weights associated with the contributing trust attributes by proposing a novel trust management mechanism that utilizes context information in addition to employing relevant impacting quantities as weights to formulate trust evaluations. Moreover, the envisaged trust management model also incorporates a) attack resilience while constituting certain parameters and b) an adaptive and flexible threshold to mitigate malevolent behavior. The simulation results depict that the devised parameters and the formulated trust aggregation cater for the dynamic nature of vehicular networks demonstrating the rationality of the weights' quantification. Furthermore, the introduction of the adaptive threshold for misbehavior detection aligns well with the requirements of the ever-changing vehicular networks.

3.1 OVERVIEW

IoV has prevailed the intelligent transportation systems owing to various distinctive characteristics such as improved safety, commercial infotainment, and efficacious traffic flows [1]. The IoV applications can be categorized in two major categories: (1) safety-critical applications, and (2) non-safety applications [2].

3.1.1 SAFETY-CRITICAL APPLICATIONS

Safety-critical applications emphasize on preventing and reducing the number of road fatalities. Such applications are proactive in nature and they operate by generating warnings and alerts for the drivers to help avert the accident. Vehicular safety-critical applications such as collision avoidance warning, emergency brake notification and right/left turn assistance demand sensitivity to real-time performance [3]. Selected examples of safety-critical applications are discussed below:

1. Collision Avoidance Warning: Such applications primarily focus on improving road safety and alleviating road accidents by preventing collisions, including collisions of vehicles with other vehicles and with pedestrians. These collisions can occur as a result of stop sign violation, traffic signal violation, and lack of pedestrian crossing information.
2. Emergency Brake Notification: These applications emphasize on preventing road crashes by notifying vehicles in case the vehicle in front of them applies brake abruptly. Such applications are particularly useful when the

DOI: 10.1201/9781032723662-3

driver has a limited visibility as a result of weather conditions or another vehicle blocking the view.

3. Right/Left Turn Assistance: Such applications mainly focus on avoiding road mishaps by providing assistance to vehicles making a turn while driving especially at an intersection. These applications acquire information from numerous sensors embedded in the vehicle itself and in its immediate ambience to aid in making turns safely.

3.1.2 NON-SAFETY APPLICATIONS

Non-safety applications focus on providing infotainment services and convenience to commuters, drivers, and passengers. The applications such as navigation systems, Internet services and file downloading services are delay and data loss tolerant. Selected examples of non-safety applications are discussed below:

1. Intelligent Parking Navigation Systems: Such applications facilitate drivers in finding and locating vacant parking spots, subsequently, helping in saving time and alleviating the amount of CO_2 emissions by getting off the road quickly. These applications are especially beneficial in peak hours.

2. File Sharing Services: These applications enable passengers to exchange data among each other by transferring pictures, audios, videos, etc. Such applications include peer to peer (P2P) applications such as bit torrent, Car-Torrent, and Fleenet, which helps improve the passengers' experience and comfort.

3. Internet Services: The unavoidable demand of the internet in our everyday lives bring forward the need to get internet service provisions for travelers on the road. Applications such as online gaming, and online video streaming takes advantage of such provisions.

3.1.3 TRUST MANAGEMENT AND CONTEXT-AWARENESS

As mentioned earlier, to tackle insider attacks on vehicular networks, the notion of trust has lately been introduced and several trust management models have been proposed [4]. Trust is defined as the belief of a vehicle (referred to as a trustor) in its peer vehicle (referred to as a trustee) relying on the past interactions among the two and the opinions towards a trustee, acquired by a trustor's neighboring vehicles. Trust computation in the said trust management models takes into account numerous parameters, e.g., quality of past interactions (i.e., packet delivery ratio), neighbor recommendations, time, distance, familiarity, frequency of interactions, etc. and amalgamate these parameters to compute the final trust value. While accumulating these parameters, weights are often associated with individual parameters to reflect their significance in the final trust score. In order to decide which vehicles are honest and which are not, a threshold is defined and vehicles having a trust value above this pre-defined threshold are categorized as trustworthy. If the trust score of a vehicle falls below the said threshold, that vehicle is identified as a malicious vehicle and information received only from a trusted vehicle is accepted.

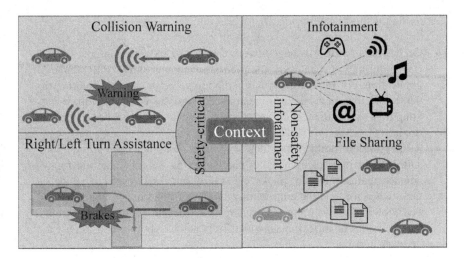

Figure 3.1   Context: Safety-critical and Non-safety (Infotainment) Applications. (Please note that the figure in the digital edition is displayed with color.)

Context can be defined as the knowledge that can prove useful in determining the circumstances of a target entity. The said entity can be an individual, a location, or an object (e.g., a vehicle) that has specific/precise relevance to the interaction among an end-user and an application, in addition to the end-user and the application [5]. Similarly, context-aware security is defined as a collection of context-specific supplementary information having relevance to the security practices concerning a certain task which aids in enhancing the security related decision making [6, 7]. Connected IoT devices are used to acquire real time context related data concerning the user's ambience. Real scenarios are transformed into information and subsequently used to offer accessible intelligence. The utilization of this information aids in achieving decision making by applications that is aligned with the decisions made by humans [8, 9]. Accordingly, we define context as the category of the communication or message exchange, i.e., safety-critical or non-safety (infotainment), among vehicles in vehicular applications during the trust evaluation process as depicted in Fig. 3.1.

Cryptography-based security solutions alone have not been effective on insider attacks and thus the notion of trust has been instituted. Substantial work has been carried out in the subject area, i.e., vehicular trust management, nevertheless, determining logical and reasonable values for the associated weights is a challenging issue that requires in-depth research. Moreover, deciding a precise value for the misbehavior detection threshold demands considerable attention as setting the value too low or too high may lead to inaccurate categorization of honest and dishonest vehicles. In addition, the consideration of historical behavior along with the introduction of an appropriate time-dependant influence and retribution for dishonest conduct in the past are essential constituents to cater for attack resistance in a trust model. Furthermore, the introduction of context information is of great significance and could enhance the trust evaluation substantially.

Accordingly, this chapter primarily focuses on:

- Orchestrating a trust management framework by incorporating the context (i.e., information regarding safety-critical and non-safety (infotainment) applications) of the communication among vehicles and by exploring diverse contributing attributes to guarantee a rigorous criterion while evaluating trust scores to meet the stringent demands of these vehicular applications;
- Addressing the problem pertinent to weight quantification by employing suitable and rational influencing parameters as weights, catering for resilience against multiple attacks, e.g., on-off attacks and selective node attacks when formulating contributing parameters, and integrating historical behavior with relevant time-aware impact besides introducing the influence of a vehicle's historical misconduct for penalizing purposes to reflect the network dynamics;
- Formulating a flexible and adaptive misbehavior detection threshold to alleviate malicious conduct while accommodating the dynamic nature of vehicular networks, furthermore, carrying out extensive simulations that demonstrate the rationality of the context-awareness, devised contributing trust parameters, weights' quantification, and the proposed adaptive threshold to cater with the requirements of the ever-changing vehicular network.

3.1.4 ORGANIZATION OF THE CHAPTER

The rest of the chapter is organized as follows. Section 3.2 provides an overview of the existing state-of-the-art trust management models. Section 3.3 discusses the system architecture and presents the mathematical details of our proposed trust management model. Section 3.4 reports the simulation setup and experimental results. Finally, Section 3.5 offers some concluding remarks.

3.2 RELATED WORK

It is worth noting that this section sheds light on the related work specific to this chapter only. An extensive review of the existing literature suggests a diverse range of trust management models in VANETs have been proposed. Chen et al. [10] suggested a trust management model reliant on blockchain for decentralized trust computation of vehicles. The proposed scheme calculates the global trust for every vehicle by computing the weighted sum of the vehicle's previous trust score, and its message sending and rating behaviors, nevertheless, the values of the weights associated with these parameters remain unexplained. Similarly, Keshavarz et al. [11] presented a trust management scheme, wherein the trust scores are computed in a centralized manner for each unmanned aerial vehicle by calculating the weighted sum of a trustee's energy consumption, its task success rate, and the path deviation. Nonetheless, the quantification of the said weights remain unexplored.

Alnasser et al. [12] proposed a trust assessment scheme, wherein the current trust and the indirect trust of a vehicle are amalgamated to compute the global trust of that vehicle. The mean of the direct trust and that of the past trust is taken as the current trust, whereas the indirect trust is the weighted sum of both, negative and positive, recommendations resulted by combining the confidence score and the global trust. This suggests that both, direct and past trusts, have an equal importance in the current trust evaluation. The global trust computation employs the notion of weights, however, the quantification of these weights remain unexplained. Wang et al. [13] presented a trust computation scheme, wherein the neighbor trust is computed as the weighted sum of the success rate and that of the packet number trust (i.e., the trust computed by the number of packets sent by a sensor node). The proposed model aggregates the sensing capability of a vehicle, its communication behaviors, and its weighted energy trust to assess the total trust of a vehicle. The authors, however, have not discussed the quantification of the associated weights. The trust management model proposed by Hasrouny et al. [14], calculates the trust score of a vehicle by aggregating the direct and the indirect trust of the vehicle evaluated by peer vehicles, group leader, and the Roadside Unit (RSU). The said assessments are performed under two scenarios, normal and event triggered. While computing the total trust score at the vehicle level, manually assigned (i.e., pre-defined) weights have been associated with the direct trust, whereas the trust score calculated at the group leader level is the mean of all the trusts computed at the vehicle level, which implies that the trust assigned by each peer has an equal influence. Moreover, the quantification of the pre-defined weights remain unexplained.

Luo et al. [15] employed equal weights for past and current behaviors to prevent trust boosting relying on recent interactions, however, assigning equal preference to both may not be a good idea for newcomers as they will not have any past behaviors to rely on, resulting in honest vehicles getting lower trust scores. Moreover, the quantification of the values defined as balancing factors has not been discussed by the authors. Li et al. [16] introduced cold start and equilibrium parameters while computing a vehicle's behavior, however, the quantification of these parameters remain unexplained. Similarly, pre-defined values for weighted factors assigned to data and control trusts have utilized by Zhang et al. [17], nevertheless, the manuscript lacks a discussion on the quantification of the same. Furthermore, the assigned values suggest an equal preference of each of these parameters which makes the idea of introducing weights meaningless. Kang et al. [18] associated pre-defined weight parameters with positive and negative interactions, historical and current interactions, reputation computation, and verifier's incentive without shedding any light on the quantification of the values of these weights. Dewanta et al. [19] evaluated the trust among a fog client vehicle and the fog service provider vehicle as the weighted sum of parameters, e.g., entity type, bidding number and record of transaction, nevertheless, the quantification of these parameters and their respective weights has not been discussed.

3.3 PROPOSED TRUST EVALUATION AND MANAGEMENT FOR IOV

The overall system architecture of the envisaged trust management model comprises vehicles interacting with other vehicles within a vehicular cluster and forming opinions about each other. Furthermore, the context of the interaction among vehicles has also been registered/considered while performing these evaluations. The said opinions are integrated and the resulting pairwise (i.e., from a trustor to a trustee), local trust along with the context-dependant trust are reported to the local authority, i.e., the roadside unit, where these assessments are combined to obtain an aggregated pairwise trust value. Subsequently, a global trust score is computed for each vehicle by accumulating these aggregated pairwise trust values to establish a single belief about each vehicle. Fig. 3.2 sketches the overall system architecture, whereas Fig. 3.3 presents the system framework of the proposed trust management model.

We define a set of vehicles Veh_v, where $v = \{1, \ldots, V''$. At every time instance k, each vehicle interacts (i.e., communicates) with other vehicles in its vicinity, and, accordingly, assess each other on the basis of the quality of interaction among them. The said assessment takes place in the form of pairs, i.e., the vehicle assessing the other vehicle is the trustor i, and the one being assessed is the trustee j ($i \neq j$), and is termed as local trust $LT_{i,j,k}$. Consequently, every trustee j is evaluated by all of its neighbors (i.e., $|v-1|$) trustors, to compute the global trust $GT_{j,k}$ of the said trustee j. Table 3.1 outlines the mathematical notations employed in the system model.

3.3.1   LOCAL TRUST

The local trust ($LT_{i,j,k}$) encompasses the weighted sum of (a) the direct trust, i.e., the direct observation of a trustor i towards a trustee j at time instance k, and (b) the indirect trust, i.e., the opinion of all the neighbors (i.e., $|v-2|$) of a trustor i towards a trustee j at time instance k.

Direct Trust ($DT_{i,j,k}$): The direct trust represents the direct opinion of a trustor i towards a trustee j based on the quality of the interaction among the two. The quality of the said interaction is measured by the packet delivery ratio (i.e., PDR) between a trustor i and a trustee j.

Packet Delivery Ratio (PDR$_{i,j,k}$) – The packet delivery ratio ($0 \leq PDR_{i,j,k} \leq 1$) represents the proportion of the successful interactions (i.e., the messages received successfully) to the total number of interactions among a trustor i and a trustee j, and is computed as:

$$PDR_{i,j,k} = \frac{s_{i,j,k}}{s_{i,j,k} + u_{i,j,k}} \tag{3.1}$$

where, $s_{i,j,k}$ represents the successful interactions from j to i at time instance k, whereas, $u_{i,j,k}$ represents the unsuccessful interactions from j to i at time instance k.

Time Decay ($\Gamma_{i,j,k}$) – The time decay ($0 \leq \Gamma_{i,j,k} \leq 1$) represents how recent the interaction among a trustor i and a trustee j is, and is computed as:

$$\Gamma_{i,j,k} = \frac{k_{int_{i,j}}}{k_{current}} \tag{3.2}$$

where, $k_{int_{i,j}}$ represents the time instance when the said interaction took place, whereas, $k_{current}$ represents the current time instance.

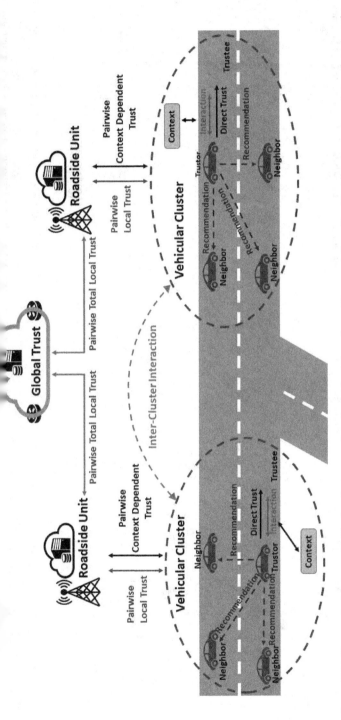

Figure 3.2 System Architecture: Vehicular clusters consist of vehicles interacting with one another, direct trust and recommendation represent the direct observation and the indirect observation of a vehicle (trustor) towards another vehicle (trustee), respectively, context defines the nature of the interaction (i.e., safety-critical or non-safety), and the roadside unit is the local authority that accumulates pairwise local and context-dependent trusts. (Please note that the figure in the digital edition is displayed with color.)

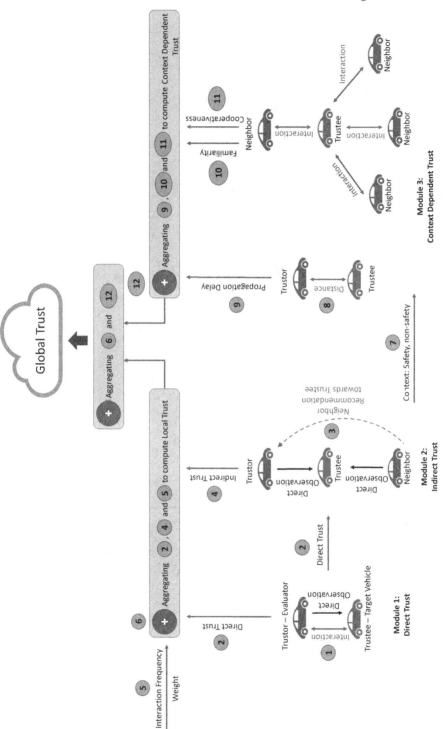

Figure 3.3 Detailed System Framework: A trustor assigns direct trust to a trustee which transforms into indirect trust for other trustors, interaction frequency specifies the weight of direct and indirect trust, context represents the nature of the interaction (i.e., safety-critical or non-safety) between a

Table 3.1
Notations & Definitions.

Notation	Definition
$|v|$	Total number of vehicles
k	Time instance
i	Trustor
j	Trustee
$LT_{i,j,k}$	Local Trust among a pair of a *Trustor* and a *Trustee*
$DT_{i,j,k}$	Direct Trust among a pair of a *Trustor* and a *Trustee*
$PDR_{i,j,k}$	Packet Delivery Ratio among a pair of a *Trustor* and a *Trustee*
$s_{i,j,k}$	Successful interactions among a pair of a *Trustor* and a *Trustee*
$u_{i,j,k}$	Unsuccessful interactions among a pair of a *Trustor* and a *Trustee*
$\Gamma_{i,j,k}$	Time Decay for an interaction among a pair of a *Trustor* and a *Trustee*
$k_{int_{i,j}}$	Time instance when the interaction took place
$k_{current}$	Current time instance
$\lambda_{i,j,k}$	Forgetting Factor
$IDT_{i,j,k}$	Indirect Trust among a pair of a *Trustor* and a *Trustee*
$\theta_{i,n,k}$	Confidence Factor among a pair of a *Trustor* and a *Neighbor*
$\beta_{i,j,k}$	Frequency of Interaction among a pair of a *Trustor* and a *Trustee*
$x_{i,j}$	Interaction among a pair of a *Trustor* and a *Trustee*
$CDT_{i,j,k}$	Context-dependant Trust among a pair of a *Trustor* and a *Trustee*
$PD_{i,j,k}$	Propagation Delay among a pair of a *Trustor* and a *Trustee*
$D_{i,j,k}$	Distance among a pair of a *Trustor* and a *Trustee*
S_p	Propagation speed
$Co_{j,k}$	Cooperativeness of a *Trustee*
$N_{j,k}$	Neighboring vehicles of a *Trustee*
$F_{i,j,k}$	Familiarity among a pair of a *Trustor* and a *Trustee*
$N_{j,k}$	Neighboring vehicles of a *Trustor*
$TLT_{i,j,k}$	Total Local Trust among a pair of a *Trustor* and a *Trustee*
$C_{txt_{i,j,k}}$	Context of communication among a pair of a *Trustor* and a *Trustee*
$GT_{j,k}$	Global Trust of a *Trustee*
V_{s_k}	Suspicious vehicle
V_{m_k}	Malicious vehicle
Th_{adapt_k}	Adaptive threshold

Forgetting Factor ($\lambda_{i,j,k}$) – The forgetting factor ($0 \leq \lambda_{i,j,k} \leq 1$) ensures that the dishonest behavior of a trustee is not easily forgotten, and is computed as:

$$\lambda_{i,j,k} = 1 - LT_{i,j,k-1} \tag{3.3}$$

where, $LT_{i,j,k-1}$ represents the local trust of trustor i towards trustee j on the previous time instance $k-1$.

As depicted in Algorithm (1), the direct trust $DT_{i,j,k}$ of a trustor i towards a trustee j at the time instance k takes into account the *PDR* amongst the two at the said time instance and the weighted sum of the *PDR* amongst the two at the earlier time instances. The *PDR* of the historical interactions is weighted w.r.t. the freshness of the particular time instances, i.e., the recent interactions are assigned higher weights as they are deemed more significant as compared to the old interactions while computing the direct trust. Furthermore, it has also been ensured that the untrustworthy behavior of a trustee is not forgotten easily by introducing a forgetting factor, i.e., the more untrustworthy behavior a trustee shows in the earlier time instance, the more it will be remembered by assigning it a higher weightage, and vice versa. The direct trust is computed as:

$$DT_{i,j,k} = \frac{(1 - \lambda_{i,j,k})PDR_{i,j,k} + \sum_{l=1}^{k-1} \Gamma_{i,j,l} PDR_{i,j,l}}{1 + \sum_{l=1}^{k-1} \Gamma_{i,j,l}} \tag{3.4}$$

where, $PDR_{i,j,k}$ represents the PDR among a trustor i and a trustee j at time instance k (Eq. 3.1), whereas, $PDR_{i,j,l}$ represents the PDR regarding the historical interactions (i.e., $1, \ldots, k-1$). Moreover, $\Gamma_{i,j,l}$ represents the weight of the specific historical interaction, i.e., the time decay factor (Eq. 3.2), whereas $\lambda_{i,j,l}$ is the forgetting factor (Eq. 3.3) to include the impact of previous untrustworthiness.

The advantage of taking the historical interactions into account is that it helps to prevent the on–off attack, wherein a vehicle switches between the attack mode and the disguise mode in order to avoid detection and possible elimination from the network.

Indirect Trust ($IDT_{i,j,k}$): The indirect trust represents the recommendation/opinion of the neighbors (i.e., $|v-2|$) of a trustor i towards a trustee j at time instance k. The said recommendation/opinion relies on the direct trust computed by the neighbor n towards a trustee j at time instance k.

Confidence Factor ($\theta_{i,n,k}$) – The confidence factor ($0 \le \theta_{i,n,k} \le 1$) represents how reliable a trustor considers its neighbor, and is computed as:

$$\theta_{i,n,k} = \frac{s_{i,n,k}}{\sum\limits_{\substack{j=1 \\ j \ne i}}^{v} s_{i,j,k}} \tag{3.5}$$

where, $s_{i,n,k}$ is the successful interactions among a trustor i and its neighbor n, whereas, $\sum_{j=1}^{v} s_{i,j,k}$, $j \ne i$ represents the successful interactions among a trustor i and all its $|v-1|$ neighbors.

As delineated in Algorithm (2), the indirect trust $IDT_{i,j,k}$ of a trustor i towards a trustee j at time instance k takes into consideration the weighted sum of the *DT* computed by each neighbor (i.e., $|v-2|$ neighbors) of a trustor towards a trustee at the said time instance. The said *DT* is weighted w.r.t. the confidence level of a trustor towards its neighbors, i.e., the more the confidence level of a trustor towards a neighbor, the more weightage is assigned to the said neighbor's opinion. The indirect trust is computed as:

$$IDT_{i,j,k} = \frac{\sum\limits_{\substack{n=1 \\ j\neq i}}^{v} \theta_{i,n,k} DT_{n,j,k}}{\sum\limits_{\substack{n=1 \\ j\neq i}}^{v} \theta_{i,n,k}}, \quad n \neq i \text{ and } n \neq j \qquad (3.6)$$

where, $\theta_{i,n,k}$ is the confidence factor of a trustor i towards its neighbor n (Eq. 3.5), whereas $DT_{n,j,k}$ represents the opinion, i.e., the direct trust of the said neighbor n towards a trustee j at time instance k (Eq. 3.4).

The advantage for taking the opinion of all neighbors into account is that it prevents from the selective node attack, wherein a node (i.e., a vehicle) switches between the honest and the dishonest behaviors while interacting with different vehicles.

Algorithm 1 Direct Trust Computation at Time k

Require: Successful Interactions $s_{i,j,k}$, Unsuccessful Interactions $u_{i,j,k}$, Interaction
    Time Instant $k_{int_{i,j}}$, Previous Local Trust $LT_{i,j,k-1}$
Ensure: Pairwise Direct Trust $DT_{i,j,k}$
 1: **for** $k \leftarrow 1$ to K **do**
 2:     **for** $i \leftarrow 1$ to V **do**
 3:         **for** $j \leftarrow 1$ to V **do**
 4:             **if** $i! = j$ **then**
 5:                 $PDR_{i,j,k} \leftarrow Packet\ Delivery\ Ratio(s_{i,j,k}, u_{i,j,k})$
 6:                 $\Gamma_{i,j,k} \leftarrow Time\ Decay(k_{int_{i,j,k}}, k_{current})$
 7:                 $\lambda_{i,j,k} \leftarrow Forgetting\ Factor(LT_{i,j,k-1})$
 8:                 **for** $l \leftarrow 1$ to $k-1$ **do**
 9:                     $H_{i,j,l} \leftarrow Historic\ PDR(PDR_{i,j,l}, \Gamma_{i,j,l}, \lambda_{i,j,l})$
10:                 **end for**
11:                 update $H_{i,j,k}$
12:             **end if**
13:             $DT_{i,j,k} \leftarrow Direct\ Trust(PDR_{i,j,k}, H_{i,j,k}, \Gamma_{i,j,k}, \lambda_{i,j,k})$
14:         **end for**
15:     **end for**
16: **end for**

Aggregation of Direct and Indirect Trust:
    The direct trust $DT_{i,j,k}$ and the indirect trust $IDT_{i,j,k}$ are aggregated to compute the local trust $LT_{i,j,k}$ of a trustor i towards a trustee j at time instance k. The said aggregation is the weighted sum of the two.

Frequency of Interaction ($\beta_{i,j,k}$) – The frequency of interaction ($0 \leq \beta_{i,j,k} \leq 1$) represents how regular a trustor and a trustee communicated, i.e., interacted, and is computed as:

$$\beta_{i,j,k} = \frac{\sum\limits_{l=1}^{k} x_{i,j,l}}{\sum\limits_{\substack{j=1 \\ j\neq i}}^{v} \sum\limits_{l=1}^{k} x_{i,j,l}} \tag{3.7}$$

where, $\sum_{l=1}^{k} x_{i,j,l}$ represents the interactions between a trustor i and a trustee j at the current and all the previous time instances, whereas $\sum\limits_{\substack{j=1 \\ j\neq i}}^{v} \sum\limits_{l=1}^{k} x_{i,j,l}$ represents the interactions between a trustor and all its $|v-1|$ neighbors at the current and all the previous time instances.

Algorithm 2 Indirect and Local Trust Computation at Time k

Require: Successful Interactions $s_{i,j,k}$, Pairwise Direct Trust $DT_{i,j,k}$, Frequency of Interaction $\beta_{i,j,k}$

Ensure: Pairwise Indirect Trust $DT_{i,j,k}$, Local Trust $LT_{i,j,k}$

1: **for** $k \leftarrow 1$ to K **do**
2:     **for** $i \leftarrow 1$ to V **do**
3:         **for** $j \leftarrow 1$ to V **do**
4:             **if** $i! = j$ **then**
5:                 **for** $n \leftarrow 1$ to V **do**
6:                     **if** $n! = i$ && $n! = j$ **then**
7:                         $\theta_{i,n,k} \leftarrow Confidence\ Factor(s_{i,n,k}, s_{i,j,k})$
8:                         $DT_{n,j,k} \leftarrow Neigh\ Recom(DT_{i,j,k})$
9:                         $IDT_{i,j,k} \leftarrow Indirect\ Trust(\theta_{i,n,k}, DT_{n,j,k})$
10:                     **end if**
11:                     update $IDT_{i,j,k}$
12:                     $LT_{i,j,k} \leftarrow Local\ Trust(DT_{i,j,k}, \beta_{i,j,k}, IDT_{i,j,k})$
13:                 **end for**
14:             **end if**
15:         **end for**
16:     **end for**
17: **end for**

The local trust $LT_{i,j,k}$ considers the frequency of interactions as the weighting factor while amalgamating the direct and the indirect trust from a trustor towards a trustee at any time instance. The rationale behind introducing the frequency of interactions as weight is that if a trustor has had significant interactions with the trustee, the trustor would be able to form an accurate opinion towards the said trustee. However, if the trustor has not interacted much with the trustee, it will rely more on the recommendations from its neighbors towards the said trustee. The local trust of a trustor i towards a trustee j at time instance k is computed as:

$$LT_{i,j,k} - \beta_{i,j,k}DT_{i,j,k} + (1 - \beta_{i,j,k})IDT_{i,j,k} \qquad (3.8)$$

where, $\beta_{i,j,k}$ is the frequency of interactions among a trustor i and a trustee j at time instance k (Eq. 3.7), whereas $DT_{i,j,k}$ and $IDT_{i,j,k}$ are the direct (Eq. 3.4) and the indirect trusts (Eq. 3.6) respectively. Equation 3.8 indicates that in the case where the trustor has had frequent interactions with the trustee, the direct trust would be assigned more weight, whereas if the trustor has had very little interaction with the trustee, it would rely more on the neighbors' opinion and consequently the weight associated with the indirect trust will have a higher value.

3.3.2 CONTEXT-DEPENDANT TRUST

The context-dependant trust encompasses the weighted sum of (a) the propagation delay, i.e., the time it will take for the message to traverse from a trustee to a trustor; (b) the cooperativeness, i.e., how cooperative a trustee is with other vehicles; and (c) the familiarity, i.e., how well a trustor knows a trustee as summarized in Algorithm (3).
   Propagation Delay ($PD_{i,j,k}$)**:** The propagation delay ($0 \leq PD_{i,j,k} \leq 1$) represents how long it takes the messages to traverse from a trustee to a trustor, and is computed as:

$$PD_{i,j,k} = \frac{D_{i,j,k}}{Sp} \qquad (3.9)$$

where, $D_{i,j,k}$ represents the distance between a trustor i and a trustee j at time instance k, whereas Sp is the propagation speed of the messages from a trustee j to a trustor i.
   Cooperativeness ($Co_{j,k}$)**:** The cooperativeness ($0 \leq Co_{j,k} \leq 1$) represents how interactive, selfish or cooperative a trustee is, and is computed as:

$$Co_{j,k} = \frac{N_{j,k}}{|v - 1|} \qquad (3.10)$$

where, $N_{j,k}$ is the set of neighbors/vehicles that a trustee j is interacting with at time instance k, whereas v is the number of vehicles in the network. It should be noted that a vehicle does not necessarily communicate/interact with all of its neighbors at every time instance.
   Familiarity ($F_{i,j,k}$)**:** The familiarity ($0 \leq F_{i,j,k} \leq 1$) represents the proportion of common neighbors a trustor and a trustee have, and is computed as:

$$F_{i,j,k} = \frac{N_{i,k} \cap N_{j,k}}{N_{i,k}} \qquad (3.11)$$

where, $N_{i,k} \cap N_{j,k}$ is set of common neighbors among a trustor i and a trustee j at time instance k, whereas $N_{i,k}$ is the neighbors of a trustor i at time instance k.

Algorithm 3 Context Dependent and Global Trust Computation at Time k

---

Require: Distance $D_{i,j,k}$, Propagation Speed S_p, Neighbors N, Context $C_{txt_{i,j,k}}$
Ensure: Pairwise Context Dependent Trust $CDT_{i,j,k}$, Global Trust $GT_{j,k}$

1: **for** $k \leftarrow 1$ to K **do**
2: 　**for** $i \leftarrow 1$ to V **do**
3: 　　**for** $j \leftarrow 1$ to V **do**
4: 　　　**if** $i! = j$ **then**
5: 　　　　$PD_{i,j,k} \leftarrow$ *Propagation Delay*$(D_{i,j,k}, S_p)$
6: 　　　　$Co_{i,j,k} \leftarrow$ *Cooperativeness*$(N_{j,k}, v)$
7: 　　　　$F_{i,j,k} \leftarrow$ *Familiarity*$(N_{i,k}, N_{j,k})$
8: 　　　　$CDT_{i,j,k} \leftarrow$ *Context Dependent Trust*$(PD_{i,j,k}, Co_{i,j,k}, F_{i,j,k})$
9: 　　　　$TLT_{i,j,k} \leftarrow$ *Total Local Trust*$(LT_{i,j,k}, C_{txt_{i,j,k}}, CDT_{i,j,k})$
10: 　　　**end if**
11: 　　**end for**
12: 　**end for**
13: 　$GT_{j,k} \leftarrow$ *Global Trust*$(GT_{i,k-1}, TLT_{i,j,k})$
14: **end for**

Aggregation of Propagation Delay, Cooperativeness, and Familiarity: The aggregation of propagation delay, cooperativeness, and familiarity to get context-dependant trust is computed as:

$$CDT_{i,j,k} = \frac{(1 - PD_{i,j,k}) + Co_{j,k} + F_{i,j,k}}{3} \tag{3.12}$$

where, $1 - PD_{i,j,k}$ is the reverse of the propagation delay, $Co_{j,k}$ is the cooperativeness, and $F_{i,j,k}$ is the familiarity among vehicles computed using Eq. 3.9, 3.10, and 3.11 respectively. This way, the lower the propagation delay and the higher the cooperativeness and familiarity between two vehicles are, the higher the context related trust is. The assignment of equal weights to all three constitutive elements (i.e., PD, Co, and F) reflects equivalent significance of each of the elements while computing CDT as they all play an equal role towards expediting the propagation of information.

3.3.3　TOTAL LOCAL TRUST

The total local trust is the pairwise Total Local Trust ($TLT_{i,j,k}$) assigned by a trustor i to a trustee j at time instance k. It takes into consideration the pairwise local trust (i.e., the amalgamation of the direct and the indirect trust), context-dependant trust (i.e., the accumulation of the propagation delay, cooperativeness, and familiarity measures), and the context information.

$$C_{txt_{i,j,k}} = \begin{cases} 0.5, & \text{if safety-critical application.} \\ 0, & \text{otherwise.} \end{cases} \tag{3.13}$$

where, $C_{txt_{i,j,k}}$ is the context of the messages exchanged among a pair of a trustor and a trustee. In this chapter, we are considering two cases of context, i.e., safety-critical application and non-safety (infotainment) application.

$$TLT_{i,j,k} = (1 - C_{txt_{i,j,k}})LT_{i,j,k} + C_{txt_{i,j,k}}CDT_{i,j,k} \qquad (3.14)$$

where, $TLT_{i,j,k}$ is the pairwise Total Local Trust assigned by a trustor i to a trustee j at time instance k. $LT_{i,j,k}$ is the pairwise local trust from trustor i to trustee j at time instance k (Eq. 3.8), whereas $CDT_{i,j,k}$ is the pairwise context-dependant trust among the same pair of vehicles (Eq. 3.12). $C_{txt_{i,j,k}}$ represents the context information of the packets exchanged between the pair (Eq. 3.13).

3.3.4 GLOBAL TRUST

The global trust is the overall trust of a trustee j in the entire network at time instance k and is computed by aggregating all the pairwise total local trusts assigned by each trustor i to a target trustee j at a specific time instance k to form a single belief about the said trustee at the specified time instance.

$$GT_{j,k} = \frac{\sum_{i=1}^{v} GT_{i,k-1} TLT_{i,j,k}}{\sum_{i=1}^{v} GT_{i,k-1}}, \ j \neq i \qquad (3.15)$$

where, $TLT_{i,j,k}$ is the pairwise Total Local Trust assigned by a trustor i to a trustee j at time instance k (Eq. 3.14), whereas $GT_{i,k-1}$ is the global trust of a trustor i at the previous time instance $k-1$.

3.3.5 MISBEHAVIOR DETECTION

In this subsection, misbehavior detection mechanism has been instituted, wherein vehicles having a global trust score less than 0.5 (i.e., the mean value of the lowest (i.e., *0*) and the highest (i.e., *1*) possible trust values, otherwise stated as the neutral trust score) are considered as suspicious vehicles V_{s_k}. An adaptive and flexible threshold is introduced to accommodate the dynamic and ever-changing nature of vehicular networks for the purpose of identification of malicious vehicles V_{m_k} among the suspicious vehicles and exterminating these dishonest vehicles from the network using Eqs. 3.16 and 3.17. The envisaged scheme provides the tagged malicious vehicles with an opportunity to redeem themselves, i.e., the tagged malicious vehicles are not eradicated the first time they are flagged, however, any subsequent tagging as malicious will eliminate such vehicles from the network. This way it is ensured that the designed model is adapting according to the network dynamics and that it does not throw any vehicles out before taking the time to observe if the vehicle has improved its behavior.

$$Th_{adapt_k} = \frac{\sum_{j=1}^{|V_{s_k}|} GT_{j,k}}{|v|} \qquad (3.16)$$

where, V_{s_k} is set of suspicious vehicles at time instance k, whereas $GT_{j,k}$ is global trust of a trustee j at time instance k (Eq. 3.15) and $|v|$ is the number of vehicles in the network.

$$V_{j,k} = \begin{cases} Suspicious \ V_{s_k}, & \text{if } 0 \leq GT_{j,k} < 0.5 \\ Trustworthy, & \text{if } Th_{adapt_k} \leq GT_{j,k} \leq 1 \\ Malicious \ V_{m_k}, & \text{if } 0 \leq GT_{j,k} < Th_{adapt_k} \end{cases} \quad (3.17)$$

3.4 SIMULATION SETUP AND RESULTS

The acquisition of the dataset utilized in this chapter comprises of an IoV-based simulator [20], wherein vehicles traverse on the road with random speeds. The said simulation runs for a duration of 30 minutes, during which the vehicles exchange packets with other vehicles in the network. For every interaction among a pair of vehicles (i.e., between a trustor and a trustee), the number of packets originated at the source vehicle is kept constant, however, the number of packets successfully received at the destination vehicle varies representing the packet delivery ratio. The context of the said interactions is also captured in terms of either safety-critical or non-safety (infotainment) applications and the context of communication among a specific pair of vehicles (i.e., a particular trustor and a particular trustee) is assumed to be constant at a given time instance. Moreover, the information regarding the time instances when a specific interaction happened, and the distance between a trustor and a trustee are also gathered, assuming the distance between a pair of vehicles remains constant throughout a given time instance. Figure 3.4 presents an illustration of the said IoV-based simulator in Java. The remaining simulations are carried out on MATLAB. Please note that Trustee 2 and Trustee 6 have been selected to present the results throughout this section based on the diversity of their behavior in the network and respective results.

Figure 3.5 presents the relation between Packet Delivery Ratio and Direct Trust assigned to Trustee 2 (Fig. 3.5a) and Trustee 6 (Fig. 3.5b) by all trustors at time in-stance 5. As shown in the figure, the Direct Trust is not merely equal to the successful message transmission among a trustor and the target trustee, but it also takes into con-sideration the forgetting factor and time decay resulting in a much constricted Direct Trust.

Figure 3.6 depicts the effects of Time Decay while computing Direct Trust for Trustee 2 (Fig. 3.6a) and Trustee 6 (Fig. 3.6b) assigned by all trustors at time in-stance 5. Taking into account the time decay factor as opposed to only computing the current successful transmission ratio among a trustor and the target trustee or simply averaging the current and all past PDRs restricts the value of DT calculated by reflecting the impact of the transmission history with reasonable influence of each.

Figure 3.7 illustrates a comparison of the Global Trust computed by introducing the Forgetting Factor, i.e., the untrustworthiness of a trustee in the past to the Global Trust calculated without taking into account the previous bad behavior of a trustee. It is evident from the figure that the injection of the past untrustworthiness influences

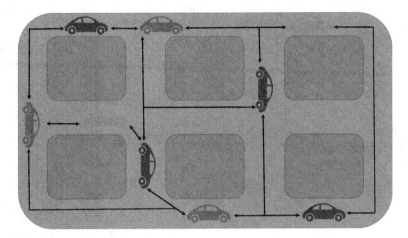

Figure 3.4 Illustration of the Simulator for the IoV Dataset. (Please note that the figure in the digital edition is displayed with color.)

and lowers the global trust of a trustee in the event of the target trustee depicting unreliable behavior.

Figure 3.8 exhibits the effect of employing context on the trust assigned to Trustee 2 (Fig. 3.8a) and Trustee 6 (Fig. 3.8b) by all trustors at time instance 5. The trust computed for safety-critical message exchange among a pair of a trustor and a trustee exerts additional parameters specific to the sensitive nature of such communication, e.g., propagation delay, familiarity, and cooperativeness resulting in a lower or a higher trust score between the said pair. For instance, Trustee 2 is more trustworthy for Trustor 3 and Trustor 5 when exchanging safety-related information whereas for

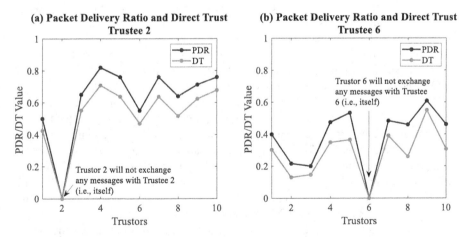

Figure 3.5 Effect – Packet Delivery Ratio and Direct Trust (Trustee 2 and Trustee 6 at Time 5). (Please note that the figure in the digital edition is displayed with color.)

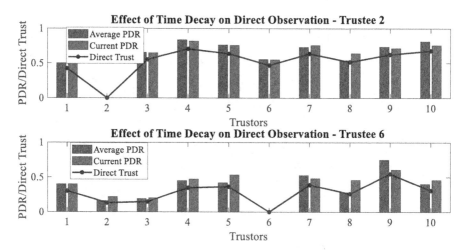

Figure 3.6 Comparison – Direct Observation with/without Time Decay (Trustee 2 and Trustee 6 at Time 5). (Please note that the figure in the digital edition is displayed with color.)

Trustor 4 and Trustor 6, it is less trustworthy. This is because of the delay between a pair as shown in Fig. 3.9, i.e., the safety-related trust is inversely proportional to the delay or distance between a trustor and a trustee. In the case of Trustee 2, the familiarity and the cooperativeness with all trustors is same at time 5 as trustee 2 is communicating with every trustor at this time instance resulting in the familiarity of 0.11 and the cooperativeness of 1.

Analogous to Fig. 3.8, Fig. 3.10 also demonstrates the impact of context information but on the overall, i.e., Global Trust of a trustee and in the form of heat maps (i.e., Fig. 3.10a for global trust with context and Fig. 3.10b for global trust without context). The introduction of context information employs a different set of parameters to compute the trust of a non-safety related message exchange as compared to the safety-related interaction. This translates to a much stringent criterion when dealing with communication regarding road safety leading to a higher/lower trust scores depending on the additional context parameters. For ease of illustration, the difference between the two heat maps has been depicted in Fig. 3.10c.

Figure 3.11 and Table 3.2 delineate comparison of the direct and indirect trust aggregation carried out by using three different approaches, BTCMV [21], the benchmark [22], and the proposed. The aggregated trust for BTCMV is computed by utilizing our dataset on Eqs.7 and 9 in [21]. The aggregated trust for Benchmark is computed by utilizing our dataset and Eqs. for DT and IDT, however, equal weights have been assigned to each of these components (as mentioned in [22] Eq. 25 and Table 2) instead of applying our computed weights. It is worth noting that while computing aggregated trust using BTCMV and the proposed scheme, the penalty factor and the forgetting factor have been ignored. Significant efforts have been made to calculate accurate values for these schemes considering the lack of information/ insufficient information in the referenced works. The pairwise aggregated trust evaluated

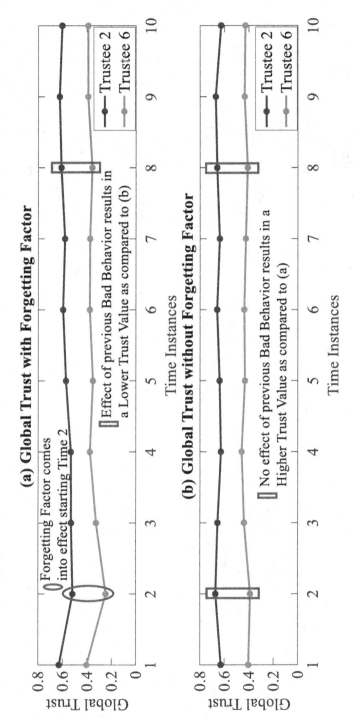

Figure 3.7 Comparison – Global Trust with/without Forgetting Factor (Trustee 2 and Trustee 6). (Please note that the figure in the digital edition is displayed with color.)

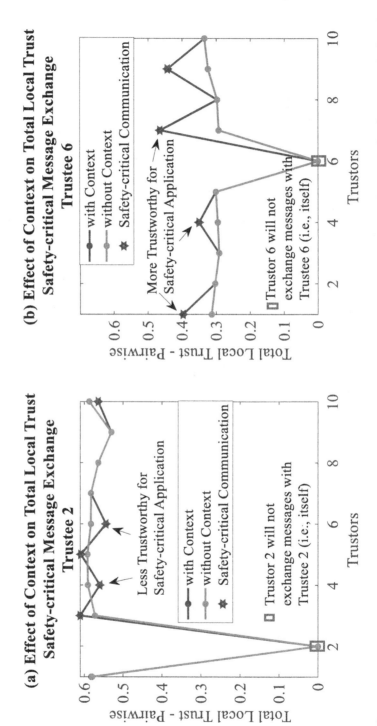

Figure 3.8 Effect of Context – Trust for Safety-critical Communication (Trustee 2 and Trustee 6 at Time 5). (Please note that the figure in the digital edition is displayed with color.)

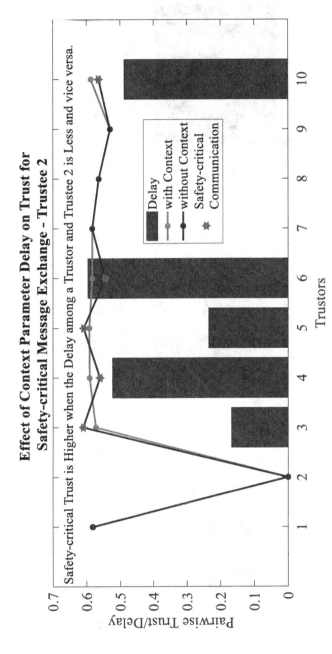

Figure 3.9 Effect of Delay – Trust for Safety-critical Communication (Trustee 2). (Please note that the figure in the digital edition is displayed with color.)

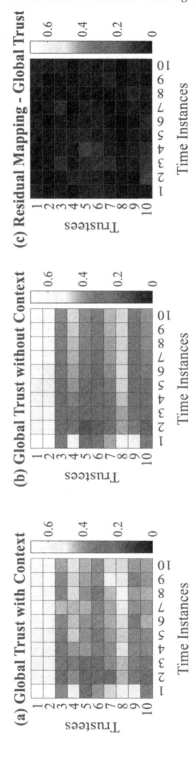

Figure 3.10 Heat Maps – (a) Global Trust with Context, (b) Global Trust without Context, and (c) Residual map – Global Trust with/without Context. (Please note that the figure in the digital edition is displayed with color.)

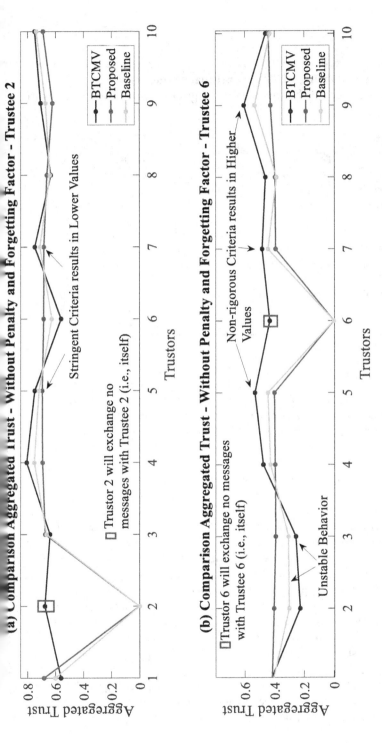

Figure 3.11 Comparison of Aggregated Trust – Employing BTCMV, Benchmark, and the Proposed Trust Evaluation Schemes. (Please note that the figure in the digital edition is displayed with color.)

Table 3.2

A Comparison – Results for Aggregated Trust of Trustee 2 and Trustee 6 – Computed by Employing BTCMV, Benchmark Scheme, and the Proposed Scheme. (Please note that the figure in the digital edition is displayed with color.)

Trustor	Aggregated Trust					
	Trustee 2			Trustee 6		
	BTCMV	Benchmark	Proposed	BTCMV	Benchmark	Proposed
1	0.5612	0.6025	0.6823	0.4253	0.4092	0.4164
2	0.6757	0	0	0.2262	0.3008	0.4030
3	0.6393	0.6638	0.6733	0.2558	0.3063	0.3916
4	0.8068	0.7525	0.6939	0.4755	0.4267	0.3956
5	0.7494	0.7196	0.6956	0.5320	0.4447	0.4004
6	0.5606	0.6272	0.6860	0.4322	0	0
7	0.7494	0.7130	0.6845	0.4837	0.4438	0.3927
8	0.6347	0.6415	0.6629	0.4614	0.3869	0.3963
9	0.7073	0.6723	0.6227	0.6060	0.5335	0.4270
10	0.7494	0.7381	0.6899	0.4605	0.4316	0.4412

by BTCMV shows that the values assigned by the trustors to trustee 2 (Fig. 3.11a) and trustee 6 (Fig. 3.11b) are significantly high reflecting non-stringent criteria for trust computations. Moreover, it evaluates a trustee even if there are no packets exchanged, e.g., it computes an aggregated trust assigned from trustor 2 to trustee 2 ignoring the fact that a vehicle will not be exchanging messages with itself. On the other hand, the baseline scheme exhibits a rather unstable behavior by reflecting the interaction quality in terms of radical trust values. Furthermore, it delegates equivalent importance to indirect observation as it does to the direct observation regardless of the number of messages exchanged among a pair of a trustor and a trustee which lacks logic and is impractical. On the contrary, the aggregated trust assessed by the proposed scheme is more rational and reasonable, and caters to the dynamic behavior of vehicles while maintaining subtle and persistent behavior.

Figure 3.12 and Table 3.3 sketch the comparison of aggregated trust evaluated utilizing BTCMV scheme employing pre-defined weights as suggested in [21] associating proposed weights (i.e., relying on the frequency of interaction among a pair of a trustor and a trustee) as recommended in this manuscript. It is evident from the figure that introducing the proposed weights in BTCMV makes the aggregated trust stable, dynamic and stringent by reflecting the quality of interactions among vehicles even when ignoring the penalty factor.

Table 3.4 outlines the comparison of the direct trust computed by RFSN [23] reported in [21] and the proposed scheme relying on the selected number of successful and unsuccessful interactions. It is apparent that RFSN relies solely on the current

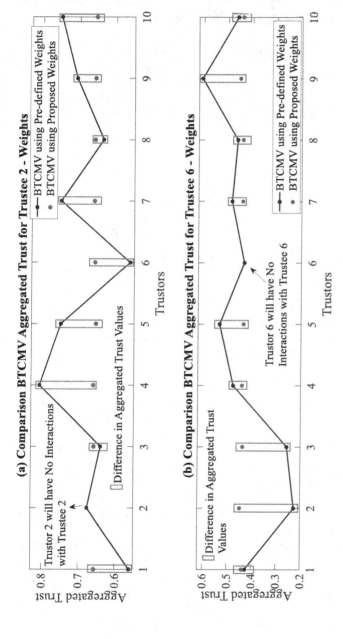

Figure 3.12 Comparison of Aggregated Trust BTCMV – Employing predefined vis-à-vis Proposed Weights. (Please note that the figure in the digital edition is displayed with color.)

Table 3.3

A Comparison – Results for Aggregated Trust of Trustee 2 and Trustee 6 – Computed by BTCMV Employing Predefined Weights to Proposed Weights.

| Trustor | BTCMV – Aggregated Trust | | | |
| | Trustee 2 | | Trustee 6 | |
	Predefined Weights	Proposed Weights	Predefined Weights	Proposed Weights
1	0.5612	0.6561	0.4253	0.4387
2	0.6757	0	0.2262	0.4469
3	0.6393	0.6578	0.2558	0.4364
4	0.8068	0.6599	0.4755	0.4394
5	0.7494	0.6536	0.5320	0.4344
6	0.5606	0.6567	0.4322	0
7	0.7494	0.6592	0.4837	0.4395
8	0.6347	0.6578	0.4614	0.4392
9	0.7073	0.6572	0.6060	0.4513
10	0.7494	0.6543	0.4605	0.4396

successful packet transmission rate among two vehicles irrespective of the increasing number of successful or unsuccessful interactions, whereas the proposed scheme takes into account other factors, e.g., the past packet delivery ratio, time decay, and forgetting factor as well to build a much dynamic and realistic model.

Figure 3.13 presents a comparison of the steady threshold utilized for malicious vehicle detection (Fig. 3.13a) to employing the proposed adaptive threshold for the same (Fig. 3.13b). The steady threshold does not cope with the dynamic demands of the vehicular network and eliminates any vehicle having a trust score below the pre-defined threshold without taking into consideration the overall network situation regarding communications. On the contrary, the proposed adaptive threshold caters for the dynamic nature of the network by accounting for the global conditions, e.g., in the event that the global trust value of each vehicle is declining, resulting from a low communication rate in the entire network, the threshold value will also decrease to avoid eradication of an honest vehicle. While in case of rise in the overall global trust, the threshold value also increases. Moreover, the proposed malicious detection mechanism provides vehicles with an opportunity to recover from bad behavior and only eliminates them from the network in case of subsequent misdemeanor. It is evident from Fig. 3.13b that the tagged vehicles at Time 2 are in fact improving their behavior and accordingly, their trust scores are recovering as well. This behavior confirms that it is of great significance to allow the tagged vehicles to rectify their situation. Another issue with pre-defined threshold is the quantification rationale. If the said threshold is kept too high, it eliminates honest vehicles as well along with the dishonest ones. On the other hand, if it is kept too low, the malicious vehicles can

Table 3.4

A Comparison of Results for Direct Trust – Computed by RFSN and the Proposed Scheme.

Trustor	$s_{i,j,k}$	$u_{i,j,k}$	Direct Trust	
			RFSN	Proposed
1	5	1	0.8333	0.8333
2	15	3	0.8333	0.7407
3	25	5	0.8333	0.7253
4	35	7	0.8333	0.7418
5	45	9	0.8333	0.7616
6	55	11	0.8333	0.7766
7	65	13	0.8333	0.7868
8	75	15	0.8333	0.7938
9	85	17	0.8333	0.7990
10	95	19	0.8333	0.8029

remain in the network undetected. Some existing research studies have suggested a threshold of 0.5 [24], whereas some defined it at 0.1 [25].

For demonstration purposes, the steady threshold in Fig. 3.13a is kept at 0.3 which is the mean of the previously discussed threshold values.

3.5 CHAPTER SUMMARY

Vehicles sharing information, both safety-critical and non-safety (infotainment), with other vehicles and their surrounding infrastructure via vehicle-to-everything (V2X) communication in Intelligent transportation systems is crucial for safe and efficient mobility. However, the participating entities are susceptible to both outsider attacks, wherein the attackers are not legitimate members of the network, and insider attacks, wherein the attackers are authorized nodes of the network. When dealing with insider attacks, the traditional cryptographic solutions alone are insufficient, consequently, the notion of trust in introduced. Accordingly, this chapter focuses on developing a trust management scheme relying on diverse influencing parameters coupled with context of the messages exchanged between vehicles. Furthermore, it addresses the challenging issue concerning weight quantification by associating rational weights computed by utilizing contributing attributes related to the network and communication dynamics. Moreover, it caters for resilience against misbehavior while formulating constituents of trust and by employing a flexible and adaptive threshold to mitigate dishonest vehicles. The dataset utilized in this chapter has been generated by employing an IoV-based simulator in Java.

The parameters involved in a trust evaluation scheme can be subjective to the dataset available, and it will be interesting and helpful to devise trust management

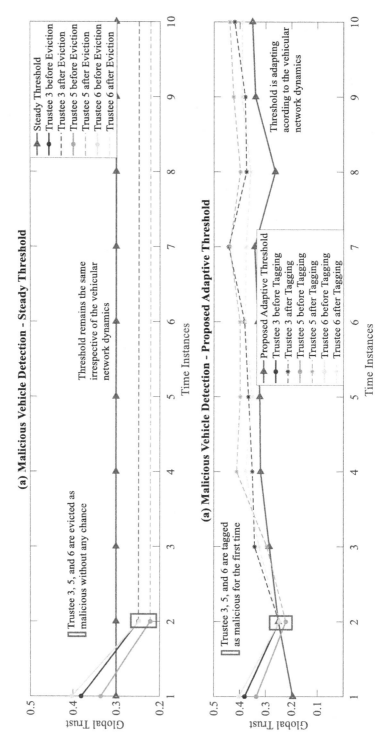

Figure 3.13 Comparison – Steady Threshold vis-à-vis Proposed Adaptive Threshold. (Please note that the figure in the digital edition is displayed with color.)

models using diverse datasets. Moreover, analyzing time-varying trust patterns to understand the suitability of each vehicle for safety-critical applications, which require real-time trustworthiness, and for non-safety application applications, which rely on the overall trustworthiness of a vehicle, is of great significance. In addition, as demonstrated earlier in this chapter (Chapter 3), it is of paramount importance to quantify weights in a way to ensure they align with the network and communication dynamics. Accordingly, the next chapter will focus on a trust management model developed by employing a different dataset, and consequently a different set of contributing parameters along with the weight quantification. Furthermore, the analysis of time-variant trust related behavior of vehicles and its suitability for specific applications for the trust evaluation scheme developed in this chapter (i.e., Chapter 3) and the one designed in the next chapter (i.e., Chapter 4) will also be discussed.

REFERENCES

1. S. A. Siddiqui, A. Mahmood, Q. Z. Sheng, H. Suzuki, and W. Ni. *A Survey of Trust Management in the Internet of Vehicles.* Electronics 10(18), 2223 (2021).
2. M. Hasan, S. Mohan, T. Shimizu, and H. Lu. *Securing Vehicle-to-Everything (V2X) Communication* (2020).
3. S. A. Siddiqui, A. Mahmood, Q. Z. Sheng, H. Suzuki, and W. Ni. *A Time-aware Trust Management Heuristic for the Internet of Vehicles.* In *2021 IEEE 20th International Conference on Trust, Security and Privacy in Computing and Communications (TrustCom)*, pp. 1–8 (IEEE, 2021).
4. W. Li and H. Song. *ART: An Attack-Resistant Trust Management Scheme for Securing Vehicular Ad Hoc Networks.* IEEE Transactions on Intelligent Transportation Systems 17(4), 960 (2016).
5. D. Grimm, M. Stang, and E. Sax. *Context-Aware Security for Vehicles and Fleets: A Survey.* IEEE Access 9, 101809 (2021).
6. V. Jovanovikj, D. Gabrijelčič, and T. Klobučar. *A Conceptual Model of Security Context.* International Journal of Information Security 13(6), 571 (2014).
7. E. de Matos, R. T. Tiburski, L. A. Amaral, and F. Hessel. *Providing Context-aware Security for IoT Environments Through Context Sharing Feature.* In *2018 17th IEEE International Conference on Trust, Security and Privacy in Computing and Communications/12th IEEE International Conference on Big Data Science and Engineering (TrustCom/BigDataSE)*, pp. 1711–1715 (2018).
8. H. J. T. Manaligod, M. J. S. Diño, S. Ghose, and J. Han. *Context Computing for Internet of Things* (2020).
9. P. Rosenberger and D. Gerhard. *Context-awareness in Industrial Applications: Definition, Classification and Use Case.*
10. X. Chen, J. Ding, and Z. Lu. *A Decentralized Trust Management System for Intelligent Transportation Environments.* IEEE Transactions on Intelligent Transportation Systems 23(1), 558 (2022).
11. M. Keshavarz, A. Shamsoshoara, F. Afghah, and J. Ashdown. *A Real-time Framework for Trust Monitoring in a Network of Unmanned Aerial Vehicles.* In *IEEE INFOCOM 2020 - IEEE Conference on Computer Communications Workshops (INFOCOM WKSHPS)*, pp. 677–682 (2020).

12. A. Alnasser, H. Sun, and J. Jiang. *Recommendation-based Trust Model for Vehicle-to-Everything (V2X)*. IEEE Internet of Things Journal 7(1), 440 (2020).
13. T. Wang, H. Luo, X. Zeng, Z. Yu, A. Liu, and A. K. Sangaiah. *Mobility based Trust Evaluation for Heterogeneous Electric Vehicles Network in Smart Cities*. IEEE Transactions on Intelligent Transportation Systems 22(3), 1797 (2021).
14. H. Hasrouny, A. E. Samhat, C. Bassil, and A. Laouiti. *Trust Model for Secure Group Leader-based Communications in VANET*. Wireless Networks 25(8), 4639 (2019).
15. B. Luo, X. Li, J. Weng, J. Guo, and J. Ma. *Blockchain Enabled Trust-based Location Privacy Protection Scheme in VANET*. IEEE Transactions on Vehicular Technology 69(2), 2034 (2020).
16. B. Li, R. Liang, D. Zhu, W. Chen, and Q. Lin. *Blockchain-based Trust Management Model for Location Privacy Preserving in VANET*. IEEE Transactions on Intelligent Transportation Systems 22(6), 3765 (2021).
17. D. Zhang, F. R. Yu, R. Yang, and L. Zhu. *Software-defined Vehicular Networks with Trust Management: A Deep Reinforcement Learning Approach*. IEEE Transactions on Intelligent Transportation Systems 23(2), 1400 (2022).
18. J. Kang, Z. Xiong, D. Niyato, D. Ye, D. I. Kim, and J. Zhao. *Toward Secure Blockchain-Enabled Internet of Vehicles: Optimizing Consensus Management Using Reputation and Contract Theory*. IEEE Transactions on Vehicular Technology 68(3), 2906 (2019).
19. F. Dewanta and M. Mambo. *Bidding Price-based Transaction: Trust Establishment for Vehicular Fog Computing Service in Rural Area*. In *2019 IEEE International Conference on Pervasive Computing and Communications Workshops (PerCom Workshops)*, pp. 882–887 (2019).
20. A. Mahmood, S. A. Siddiqui, Q. Z. Sheng, W. E. Zhang, H. Suzuki, and W. Ni. *Trust on Wheels: Towards Secure and Resource Efficient IoV Networks*. Computing pp. 1–22 (2022).
21. H. Gao, C. Liu, Y. Yin, Y. Xu, and Y. Li. *A Hybrid Approach to Trust Node Assessment and Management for VANETs Cooperative Data Communication: Historical Interaction Perspective*. IEEE Transactions on Intelligent Transportation Systems pp. 1–10 (2021).
22. S. Oubabas, R. Aoudjit, J. J. P. C. Rodrigues, and S. Talbi. *Secure and Stable Vehicular Ad Hoc Network Clustering Algorithm based on Hybrid Mobility Similarities and Trust Management Scheme*. Vehicular Communications 13, 128 (2018).
23. S. Ganeriwal, L. K. Balzano, and M. B. Srivastava. *Reputation-based Framework for High Integrity Sensor Networks*. ACM Transactions on Sensor Networks (TOSN) 4(3), 1 (2008).
24. F. Ahmad, F. Kurugollu, C. A. Kerrache, S. Sezer and L. Liu. *NOTRINO: A NOvel Hybrid TRust Management Scheme for INternet-of-Vehicles*. IEEE Transactions on Vehicular Technology 70(9), 9244 (2021).
25. A. Mahmood, B. Butler, W. E. Zhang, Q. Z. Sheng and S. A. Siddiqui. *A Hybrid Trust Management Heuristic for VANETs*. In *2019 IEEE International Conference on Pervasive Computing and Communications Workshops (PerCom Workshops)*, pp. 748–752 (2019).

4 Time-aware Trust Management for the Internet of Vehicles

The aim of this chapter is to develop a trust management model employing a different dataset, i.e., a real IoT dataset, and to analyze the time-based behavior of the aggregated trust along with the contributing parameters to study the behavior of each vehicle and to identify suitable trust-based patterns for safety-critical and non-safety vehicular applications. Moreover, pursuant to the dataset utilized, it takes into consideration a limited number of influencing trust parameters as compared to the previous chapter (i.e., Chapter 3) and addresses the challenges of quantification of the said attributes and the weights associated with these parameters, subsequently, quantifying the aggregated trust. Performance analysis demonstrates that the trust values computed via the envisaged trust model in this chapter are lower than those calculated via the benchmark scheme.

4.1 OVERVIEW

For insider attacks, i.e., the attacks launched by vehicles that have successfully completed the authentication process, the notion of trust, an extended version of the conventional trio of privacy, security, and reliability, is often introduced. The trust-based decision making is required to take place at the node level, i.e., each node should participate in the trust computations in order to support these decentralized networks. Trust aids in mitigating the perception of uncertainty and the prospective risks prior to taking any actions [1]. Trust itself is an amalgamation of a variety of trust indicators between the evaluator, commonly known as the trustor, and the one being evaluated, referred to as a trustee or a target node, including, but not limited to, the occurrence of previous and current communications among the nodes (direct observation), and the existence of the neighbor recommendations about the target node (indirect observation) [2]. In order to compute the local trust score for each vehicle, these indicators are aggregated and the recommendation of the serving local authority or the Roadside Unit (RSU) for the trustee is also considered while aggregating the final trust of the vehicle in the network, referred to as the global trust [3]. While designing the aforementioned trust management models, in order to aggregate the trust parameters to acquire a final trust score for a trustee, the contributing parameters are averaged out which implies that each factor has the same impact on the final trust score. Alternatively, the notion of weights is commonly applied, wherein different contributing parameters are assigned different weightage relying on their respective contribution in the final trust value computation [5, 4]. Nevertheless, quantifying the trust parameters and defining the value of the weights associated with these contributing parameters remain a challenge. It is pertinent to note that the development of trust management frameworks is subjective to the information available regarding the interactions among different nodes and the network dynamics (i.e., the dataset).

Time series is defined as the values against a variable that are orderly sequenced at regular intervals of time. Time-based analysis takes into consideration the fact that the information captured in the course of time, i.e., in the form of data points, hold a pattern or in other words, a relationship, e.g., periodic trend or auto-correlation. Time-based models help understand the underlying relationships that resulted in the available data output prior to applying suitable modelling techniques, according to the users' preference and application, for monitoring, predicting, and feedback control, e.g., inventory studies, budgetary analysis, sales forecasting [6]. Time series analysis is exceptionally beneficial in traffic related problems such as congestion. A wide range of solutions have been proposed to alleviate traffic congestion in urban areas, including, but not limited to, offering route navigation, upgrading transport and road infrastructure, and exercising traffic control. Route navigation alone can only help enough considering the exponentially increasing number of vehicles on the road. It is infeasible to elevate the infrastructure time and again specially when there is no room left for additional road facilities. One practical solution to mitigate this congestion is by implementing and reinforcing digitized intelligent traffic management measures. Forecasting short-term traffic flows is one of the fundamental aspects of such intelligent systems as the efficacy of these systems rely on the accuracy of traffic flow predictions [7]. Similarly, time-series data analysis can prove useful in other traffic and road concerning domains such as application (i.e., safety-critical and non-safety) based communication among vehicles. It would be impractical to believe that every vehicle in a vehicular network is equally reliable for all types of communications. Some interactions among vehicles on the road are more crucial to road safety as compared to others and in the same way, some vehicles are more dependable than their peers concerning such sensitive information.

As mentioned earlier, time-based analysis helps understand and estimate patterns of complex relationships among participating quantities. It would be beneficial to evaluate the vehicles' credibility and based on the time-based trend of these assessments, determine the suitability of different vehicles for specific applications (i.e., safety-critical and non-safety). Vehicular safety-critical applications such as collision warning, emergency brake notification and traffic congestion warning demand sensitivity to real-time performance, whereas non-safety applications such as locating fuel stations, Internet services and location prediction services make use of the overall performance patterns of the nodes. Extensive research has been performed on the steady-state analysis, however, time-varying trends need further investigation [8].

Accordingly, the main contributions of this chapter are:

- Development of a trust management model utilizing a different dataset (i.e., a real IoT dataset) for the quantification of trust score by quantifying the contributing parameters (i.e., familiarity, packet delivery ratio, timeliness, and interaction frequency) which helps translate the confidence level on a target vehicle into a number in the range of [0, 1]. These contributing parameters have been selected after thorough analysis of the communication (i.e., message exchange) amongst nodes in reference to the dataset;

- Quantification of the weights is realized by using two of the trust indicators, i.e., timeliness and interaction frequency, as the weight for packet delivery ratio and familiarity, respectively, in the process of trust aggregation to contemplate the significance of the respective contributing parameters;
- Analysis of the time-varying patterns of the aggregated trust along with the contributing parameters for both, the trust evaluation scheme envisaged in Chapter 3 and the one devised in this chapter to study the behavior of each vehicle and to identify suitable trust-based patterns for safety-critical and non-safety vehicular applications.

4.1.1   ORGANIZATION OF THE CHAPTER

The rest of the chapter is organized as follows. Section 4.2 provides an overview of the existing state-of-the-art trust management models. Section 4.3 discusses the details of our proposed trust management model. Section 4.4 reports the simulation setup and experimental results. Finally, Section 4.5 offers some concluding remarks.

4.2   RELATED WORK

A comprehensive analysis of the existing literature exhibits a variety of research studies suggesting the trust management frameworks in a VANET environment. Gao et al. [9] proposed a hybrid trust assessment scheme that combined the direct and the recommendation trust to evaluate the integrated trust of a vehicle relying on historical information regarding interactions among different vehicles. Moreover, Bayesian inference has also been employed while computing the direct trust and penalties have been imposed dynamically. In addition, the notion of sliding time window has also been introduced while computing the said trust values. While computing the integrated trust score, weighted average of the direct trust and the recommendation trust has been calculated, however, the weights utilized remain unexplained which influences the quantification of the final trust value. Furthermore, the application specific reliability and the related trust trends have not been discussed. Chen et al. [10] employed the notion of blockchain in order to carry out trust evaluation of vehicles in a decentralized manner, wherein the global trust of each vehicle is the weighted sum of the vehicle's message rating behavior, message sending behavior and that of its previous trust value, however, the weights corresponding to each of these components remain unexplained.

Similarly, Zhang et al. [11] also introduced blockchain to assess the reliability of the information exchanged among vehicles, identify dishonest vehicles disseminating malicious information, and subsequently impose penalties that negatively impact the reputation of such vehicles. However, the quantification and the decision on the values of the weights defined for computing the credibility of the data, penalty, reward, and the influence on the reputation score, etc. remain unexplained. Furthermore, the authors have not discussed the time-based trends of the credibility of the information dispersed by vehicles. Ahmad et al. [12] presented a multi-step hybrid trust evaluation framework that evaluates the credibility of the sender prior to the reliability of the information disseminated by that vehicle provided that the said vehicle is identified as trustworthy. Several parameters have been defined to perform the aforementioned evaluations, e.g., the antenna heights of both the trustor and the trustee, and the distance among them, quality of information, role-dependent trust, and the effective distance, however, the quantification of the predefined values for most of these parameters, the penalty and reward factors, along with the time-based variations in the evaluations have not been discussed by the authors.

Xia et al. [13] computed the overall trust score by computing the weighted sum of the subjective trust, i.e., the assessment of the previous interactions, and the recommendation trust, i.e., the opinions from the neighbors. The weights have been defined in detail, however, the suggested trust model lacks the time-based analysis of the vehicles' behavior. Similarly, Zhang et al. [14] presented an attack resistant trust evaluation model that computes the vehicles' local trust by employing Bayesian inference prior to evaluating the global trust of the same vehicles utilizing TrustRank algorithm. Moreover, parameters related to the behavior of the vehicles' driver and the vehicle itself are taken into account while computing the above mentioned trust scores. The quantification of the parameters and those of the associated weights have been discussed in detail, however, the authors have not discussed the trends of the computed trust scores over time.

Existing literature demonstrates a considerable amount of research in the context of trust management models. Nevertheless, they do not address the challenges pertinent to quantification of trust and that of the corresponding weights associated with the contributing parameters during the trust aggregation process. Furthermore, the time-based patterns of the trust and its contributing parameters need to be analyzed to understand the individual impact of each trust indicator as well as that of timeliness in depth, and to study the behavior of each vehicle to identify suitable trust-based patterns for safety-critical and non-safety vehicular applications.

4.3 SYSTEM MODEL

Vehicles (trustors; $m = 1,\ldots,N$) interact with their peer vehicles (trustees; $n = 1,\ldots,N$; $m \neq n$) and accordingly, compute four trust attributes namely Familiarity ($FMR_{m,n}$), Packet Delivery Ratio ($PDR_{m,n}$), Timeliness ($TML_{m,n}$), and Interaction Frequency ($IFR_{m,n}$) for each interaction $i_{m,n}$ amongst a trustor m and a trustee n using Eqs. 4.1–4.4, respectively, for the trust computation of a trustor m towards a trustee n. Table 4.1 outlines the mathematical notations employed in the system model.

Familiarity ($FMR_{m,n}$): Familiarity ($0 \leq FMR_{m,n} \leq 1$) represents the extent of a trustor's acquaintance with a trustee. It is defined in the literature as the prior knowledge regarding a target vehicle and is computed as a combination of belief, disbelief

Table 4.1

Notations & Definitions.

Notation	Definition
N	Total number of vehicles
m	Trustor
n	Trustee
$i_{m,n}$	Interaction among a pair of a *Trustor* and a *Trustee*
$FMR_{m,n}$	Familiarity among a pair of a *Trustor* and a *Trustee*
$Neigh_n$	Total number of neighbors of a *Trustee*
$Neigh_m$	Total number of neighbors of a *Trustor*
$PDR_{m,n}$	Packet Delivery Ratio among a pair of a *Trustor* and a *Trustee*
$Msg_{m,n}$	Successful message transmission from a *Trustee* to a *Trustor*
Msg_{m_n}	Total number of messages sent from a *Trustee* to a *Trustor*
$TML_{m,n}$	Timeliness of the interaction among a *Trustee* and a *Trustor*
$T_{int_{m,n}}$	Time instance when the interaction took place
$T_{current}$	Current time instance
$IFR_{m,n}$	Interaction frequency among a *Trustee* and a *Trustor*
w_{PDR}	Weight associated with PDR
w_{FMR}	Weight associated with FMR
$Trust_{p_{m,n}}$	Pairwise trust of a *Trustor* towards a *Trustee*
$Trust_n$	Global trust of a *Trustee*

and uncertainity [15]. In our proposed work, familiarity refers to the proportion of the neighbors that a trustor shares with a trustee and is computed as:

$$FMR_{m,n} = \frac{Neigh_m \cap Neigh_n}{Neigh_m} \tag{4.1}$$

where, $Neigh_m \cap Neigh_n$ is the number of common neighbors between a trustor and a trustee, and $Neigh_m$ is the total number of neighbors of a trustor. If a vehicle m (i.e., the trustor) knows a vehicle n (i.e., the trustee) quite well, it hence corresponds to a higher familiarity score and vice versa.

Packet Delivery Ratio ($PDR_{m,n}$)**:** The packet delivery ratio ($0 \leq PDR_{m,n} \leq 1$) is defined in the literature as the proportion of the generated data packets that is accurately and completely delivered [16]. In our proposed work, packet delivery ratio represents the proportion of the messages received by a trustor and is computed as:

$$PDR_{m,n} = \frac{Msg_{m,n}}{Msg_{m_n}} \tag{4.2}$$

where, $Msg_{m,n}$ is the number of messages sent by a trustee n that were successfully received by a trustor m, and Msg_{m_n} is the total number of messages sent to m by n. If a vehicle m (i.e., the trustor) has a good connection with a vehicle n (i.e., the trustee), it corresponds to a higher packet delivery ratio and vice versa.

Timeliness ($TML_{m,n}$): The timeliness ($0 \leq TML_{m,n} \leq 1$) relates to how recent the interaction amongst a trustor m and a trustee n is. In other words, timeliness is the ratio of the time instance when the interaction amongst a trustor m and a trustee n transpired vis-à-vis the current time and is computed as:

$$TML_{m,n} = \frac{T_{int_{m,n}}}{T_{current}} \tag{4.3}$$

where, $T_{int_{m,n}}$ is the time instance when the interaction amongst vehicles m and n took place and $T_{current}$ is the latest time instance. If two vehicles m and n (i.e., where m is a trustor and n is a trustee) interacted quite recently, it corresponds to a higher timeliness score and vice versa.

Interaction Frequency ($IFR_{m,n}$): The interaction frequency ($0 \leq IFR_{m,n} \leq 1$) relates to the proportion of interactions that occurred between a trustor m and a trustee n to the total number of interactions the trustor m has had and is computed as:

$$IFR_{m,n} = \frac{\sum i_{m,n}}{\sum\limits_{\substack{n=1 \\ n \neq m}}^{N-1} i_{m,n}} \tag{4.4}$$

where, $i_{m,n}$ is the interaction between a trustor m and a trustee n. Once the attributes are computed individually, the pairwise trust $Trust_{p_{m,n}}$ is calculated by utilizing timeliness ($TML_{m,n}$) and interaction frequency ($IFR_{m,n}$) as the weights for PDR and FMR, respectively, for the corresponding pair (i.e., interaction) of vehicles using:

$$Trust_{p_{m,n}} = w_{PDR}{}^{*}PDR_{m,n} + w_{FMR}{}^{*}FMR_{m,n} \tag{4.5}$$

$$w_{PDR} = \frac{TML_{m,n}}{TML_{m,n} + IFR_{m,n}} \tag{4.6}$$

$$w_{FMR} = \frac{IFR_{m,n}}{IFR_{m,n} + TML_{m,n}} \tag{4.7}$$

where, the sum of the weights associated with Familiarity and Packet Delivery Ratio is equal to 1.

Subsequently, an aggregated (global) trust score $Trust_n$ for each trustee n is calculated by taking the average of the pairwise trust $Trust_{p_{m,n}}$ evaluations of all the trustors (i.e., $N-1$ vehicles) towards a trustee n :

$$Trust_n = \frac{1}{N} \sum\limits_{\substack{m=1 \\ m \neq n}}^{N-1} Trust_{p_{m,n}} \tag{4.8}$$

The objective of weight quantification is achieved by using Eqs. 4.6–4.7, whereas Eqs. 4.1–4.2 address the quantification of the contributing parameters of familiarity

(Eq. 4.1) and packet delivery ratio (Eq. 4.2), and Eq. 4.5 addresses the trust quantification.

If a vehicle m has a significant number of common neighbors with a vehicle n but the interactions amongst m and n are less frequent, the weight for the FMR will ensure that the impact of FMR in the aggregated trust is decreased as interaction among vehicles is the key. Eventually, the parameter PDR and the weight associated with the FMR make sure that interaction amongst peers is of paramount importance while computing trust, however, if a trustor does not have a significant number of interactions with the target trustee, it is still able to calculate the trust of the said trustee by utilizing familiarity.

4.4   SIMULATION SETUP AND RESULTS

In this section, we first discuss the simulation setup and time-varying trust patterns of the nodes employing the trust management model developed in this chapter. To facilitate the reader, we will refer to the said model (i.e., proposed in this chapter) as *TMF2*. Later on in this section, we will analyze the time-based behavior of the vehicles utilizing the trust evaluation framework proposed in Chapter 3 and to make it easy for the reader, we will refer to this trust model as *TMF1*.

4.4.1   SIMULATION SETUP AND RESULTS FOR TMF2

The simulations for the proposed trust model utilize the real IoT dataset from CRAW-DAD[1] that encompasses information regarding 18,226 interactions among 76 IoT devices (nodes), both honest and dishonest, at certain time instances. The details related to the said interactions are acquired in the form of friends, the messages exchanged (i.e., both transmitted and received) and the status of these messages, activities and their duration, proximity, and interests that the said nodes share. The said simulations have been carried out in MATLAB. As delineated in Algorithm 4, the interactions between vehicles, i.e., the trustors and the trustees, have been divided into four segments according to the percentage of recent interactions, i.e., (i) 25% recent interactions, (ii) 50% recent interactions, (iii) 75% recent interactions, and (iv) all (i.e., 100%) the interactions. Subsequently, the aggregated trust and the corresponding FMR and PDR for each of the four segments are computed. Tables 4.2, 4.3, and 4.4 depict the aggregated trust, FMR, and PDR trends over time, respectively, for selected vehicles (i.e., vehicle no. 3, 32, and 49).

Figure 4.1 depicts the normalized Aggregated Trust, normalized FMR, and normalized PDR for all 76 nodes with respect to the recent 25% (illustrated in column 1), 50% (illustrated in column 2), 75% (illustrated in column 3), and 100% interactions (illustrated in column 4) among the nodes. The normalized values for Aggregated Trust, FMR, and PDR have been utilized to rescale the respective values on a scale of *0* to *1* for the sake of visibility. The depicted Aggregated Trust (illustrated

---

[1]https://ieee-dataport.org/open-access/crawdad-thlabsigcomm2009

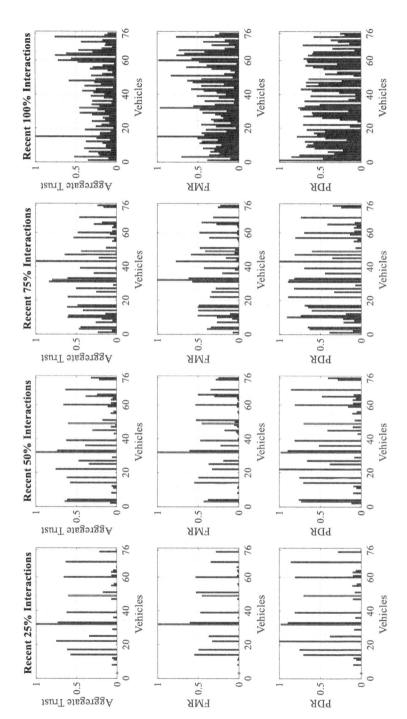

Figure 4.1 Time-varying Patterns for Trust, Familiarity, and Packet Delivery Ratio of all 76 Vehicles with respect to Percentage Recent Interactions (red color represents vehicle no. 3, magenta color represents vehicle no. 32, whereas green color represents vehicle no. 49). (Please note that the figure in the digital edition is displayed with color.)

Algorithm 4 Trust Computation TMF2 w.r.t. % Recent Interactions.

Require: Common Neighbors $Neigh_{m,n}$, Trustor's Neighbors $Neigh_m$, Successful
Messages $Msg_{m,n}$, Total Messages Msg_{m_n}, Current Time Instance $T_{current}$, Interaction Time Instance $T_{int_{m,n}}$, Interaction $i_{m,n}$, Trustor's Total Interactions i_m

Ensure: Aggregated Trust Percentage Interaction $Trust_n x\%$

1: **for** $m \leftarrow 1$ to N **do**
2:     **for** $n \leftarrow 1$ to N **do**
3:         $FMR_{m,n} \leftarrow Familiarity(Neigh_{m,n}, Neigh_m)$
4:         $PDR_{m,n} \leftarrow Packet\ Delivery\ Ratio(Msg_{m,n}, Msg_{m_n})$
5:         $TML_{m,n} \leftarrow Timeliness(T_{current}, T_{int_{m,n}})$
6:         $IFR_{m,n} \leftarrow Interaction\ Frequency(i_{m,n}, i_m)$
7:     **end for**
8: **end for**
9: **for** $x \leftarrow 0\%$ to 100% **do**
10:     $Threshold \leftarrow (1 - x)^* RangeTime$
11:     **for** $m \leftarrow 1$ to N **do**
12:         **for** $n \leftarrow 1$ to N **do**
13:             **if** $TML_{m,n} \geq Threshold$ **then**
14:                 $Trust_{p_{m,n}} x\% \leftarrow Agg(FMR_{m,n}, PDR_{m,n}, TML_{m,n}, IFR_{m,n})$
15:             **else**
16:                 $Trust_{p_{m,n}} x\% \leftarrow 0$
17:             **end if**
18:         **end for**
19:     **end for**
20:     $Trust_n x\% \leftarrow sum(Trust_{p_{m,n}} x\%)$
21: **end for**

---

in row 1) is the weighted sum of FMR and PDR computed via Eq. 4.8. Moreover,
FMR is depicted (illustrated in row 2) for each vehicle having interaction segments
in the timeliness intervals [0.25, 1] for recent 75% interactions, [0.5, 1] for recent
50% interactions, [0.75, 1] and [0, 1] for recent 25% and 100% interactions, respectively. Similarly, the PDR (illustrated in row 3) is also illustrated for each vehicle
for the said interaction segments. As we increase the time range to be included in
the trust computations, the figures become more and more populated as the number
of vehicles interacting and the number of interactions are growing. For instance, the
aggregated trust of vehicle no. 3 has a value of zero when aggregated for the recent
25% interactions. This is because the said vehicle has not initiated any interactions
in the most recent time window, i.e., [0.75, 1] resulting in the FMR and the PDR
of zero. On the contrary, vehicle no. 32 shares common neighbors with a significant
number of trustors (i.e., 41 other vehicles/trustors) and depicts the second best PDR
in the network resulting in the highest trust among all its peers during the most recent time window, i.e., [0.75, 1]. Similarly, vehicle no. 49 shares neighbors with a
good number of vehicles (i.e., 27 trustors), and further initiates a good number of

Table 4.2
Aggregated Trust Trend over Time.

Vehicle No.	25%	50%	75%	100%
3	0	0.6418	0.4667	0.5176
Neighbors	0	26	26	50
Successful Interactions	0	92	141	156
32	1	1	0.7938	0.4539
Neighbors	41	41	48	58
Successful Interactions	145	194	316	412
49	0.6008	0.6008	0.4369	0.2506
Neighbors	27	27	27	43
Successful Interactions	61	76	76	131

successful interactions (i.e., 61 interactions) with its neighboring vehicles resulting in a significant PDR, and a good aggregated trust score. The aggregated trust for vehicle no. 3 has a significant value when accumulating 50%, 75%, or 100% interactions as compared to the aggregated trust when aggregating recent 25% interactions which

shows that the said vehicle has initiated a good number of successful interactions, i.e., 92, 141, and 156 in the time windows [0.5, 1], [0.25, 1] and [0, 1], respectively. Furthermore, it shares a good number of neighbors, i.e., 26, 26, and 50 with other vehicles in the time windows [0.5, 1], [0.25, 1] and [0, 1], respectively. Similarly, vehicle no. 49 has a higher aggregated trust value for recent 25% and 50% interactions as compared to recent 75% interactions due to a decrease in the FMR and PDR scores. This shows that the said vehicle has better quality interactions (i.e., in terms of packet dropping and the number of shared neighbors in the network) with neighboring vehicles most recently.

Figure 4.2 illustrates the comparison of the aggregated trust (non normalized) computed by the proposed trust management model (illustrated in row 1) vis-á-vis the aggregated trust (non normalized) calculated by a benchmark trust evaluation scheme (illustrated in row 2). The said benchmark scheme computes the aggregated trust by associating an equal weight of 0.5 with each of the two parameters. The non normalized values are utilized as the objective here is to compare the absolute values of Trust computed for each vehicle via the two methods. It is evident that the trust scores computed by the proposed trust management model have considerably lower values than the trust scores computed by the benchmark scheme. This implies that the proposed model employs a vigorous criterion to compute aggregated trust that ensures timely identification of the malicious vehicles (i.e., the vehicles having a trust score below a predefined threshold) as it does not allow the vehicles to gain/improve

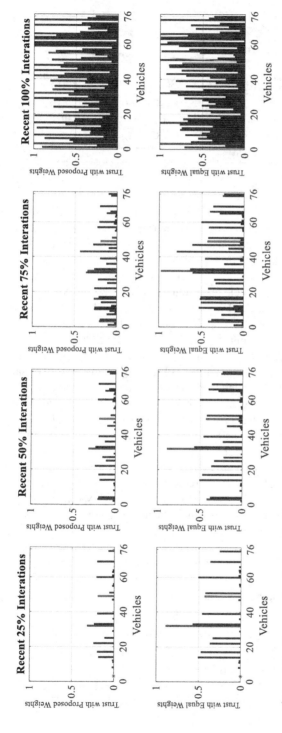

Figure 4.2 Time-varying Patterns for Trust ascertained via Envisaged Scheme vis-á-vis Trust-based Benchmark Schemes, i.e., Assigning Equal Weights to the Contributing Parameters (red color represents vehicle no. 3, magenta color represents vehicle no. 32, whereas green color represents vehicle no. 49). (Please note that the figure in the digital edition is displayed with color.)

Table 4.3
Familiarity Trend over Time.

Vehicle No.	25%	50%	75%	100%
3	0	0.4307	0.391	0.7016
32	1	1	1	0.9643
49	0.453	0.453	0.4113	0.4546

trust easily.

As mentioned earlier in Section 4.1, safety-critical vehicular applications make decisions over the instantaneous trust, whereas non-safety vehicular applications require over time patterns for decision making. Accordingly, Figure 4.3 depicts the time-varying trust patterns of three vehicles. Figure 4.3(a) delineates the patterns of vehicle no. 33 and it can be observed that trust aggregating the most recent interactions (i.e., 25%) for this vehicle is quite high. Therefore, this vehicle is trustworthy when it comes to safety-critical vehicular applications. The said vehicle may also be reliable for non-safety vehicular applications as its trust is improving over time and becoming stable. Similarly, Figure 4.3(b) illustrates the patterns of vehicle no. 48 and it can be observed that the trust accumulating the most recent interactions (i.e., 25%) of this vehicle is quite low making this vehicle highly unreliable for safety-critical vehicular applications. Although there is a drastic increase in the trust when accumulating 100% interactions, the unstable behavior of the vehicle makes it unreliable for non-safety vehicular applications as well. Furthermore, Figure 4.3(c) demonstrates the behavioral patterns of vehicle no. 51 and it can be seen that the said vehicle has a rather stable trust score over time, however, the trust scores are quite low and the behavior of the vehicle over time tends to be selfish as there is a sudden drop in the trust score when 75% recent interactions are computed which confirms that this vehicle is unreliable for both safety-critical and non-safety vehicular applications.

To recall the simulation setup from Chapter 3, a set of vehicles Veh_v, where

Table 4.4
Packet Delivery Ratio Trend over Time.

Vehicle No.	25%	50%	75%	100%
3	0	0.7334	0.6298	0.8513
32	0.9823	0.9823	0.8841	0.7681
49	0.702	0.702	0.6028	0.641

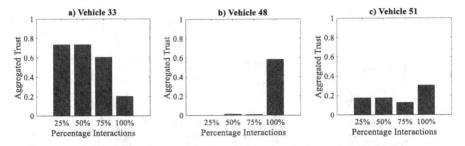

Figure 4.3 Aggregated Trust Variation over Time for a) Vehicle no. 33, b) Vehicle no. 48, and c) Vehicle no. 51. (Please note that the figure in the digital edition is displayed with color.)

$v = \{1, \ldots, V''$ is defined. At every time instance k, each vehicle interacts (i.e., communicates) with other vehicles in its vicinity, and, accordingly, assess each other on the basis of the quality of interaction among them. The said assessment takes place in the form of pairs, i.e., the vehicle assessing the other vehicle is the trustor i, and the one being assessed is the trustee j $(i \neq j)$, and is termed as local trust $LT_{i,j,k}$. Consequently, every trustee j is evaluated by all of its neighbors (i.e., $|v-1|$) trustors, to compute the global trust $GT_{j,k}$ of the said trustee j. The interactions between vehicles, i.e., the trustors and the trustees, have been divided into four segments according to the percentage of recent interactions, i.e., (i) 25% recent interactions, (ii) 50% recent interactions, (iii) 75% recent interactions, and (iv) all (i.e., 100%) the interactions. Subsequently, the global trust and the corresponding DT, IDT and CDT for each of the four segments are computed. Algorithm 5 depicts the said approach and simulations.

4.4.2   SIMULATION SETUP AND RESULTS FOR TMF1

Figure 4.4 depicts the normalized Global Trust, normalized direct trst (DT), normalized indirect trust (IDT), and normalized context dependent trust (CDT) for all 10 vehicles with respect to the recent 25% (illustrated in column 1), 50% (illustrated in column 2), 75% (illustrated in column 3), and 100% interactions (illustrated in column 4) among the nodes. The normalized values for Global Trust, DT, IDT, and CDT have been utilized to rescale the respective values on a scale of 0 to 1 for the sake of visibility. The depicted Global Trust (illustrated in row 1) has been computed via Eq. 3.15, whereas the DT, IDT, and CDT (illustrated in row 2, 3, and 4, respectively) have been calculated via Eqs. 3.4, 3.6, and 3.12. Equation 3.4 yields pairwise DT among a trustor and a trustee, therefore, to compute a composite DT for each vehicle (i.e., trustee), an average of the DT assigned to each vehicle by all the trustors has been calculated and depicted in the figure. Similarly, the IDT and CDT resulting via 3.6, and 3.12 are also pairwise values, therefore, the same process has been applied on them and presented in the figure. The global trust of vehicle no. 1 has a higher value when aggregated for the recent 25% and 50% interactions as compared to the 75% and 100% recent interactions which reflect that the said vehicle has initiated reliable

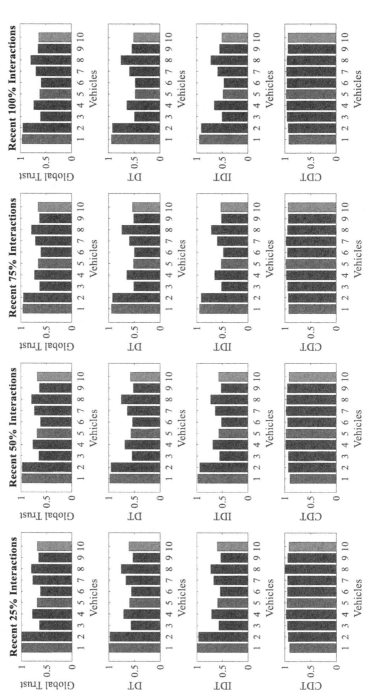

Figure 4.4 Time-varying Patterns for Global Trust, Direct Trust, Indirect Trust, and Context Dependent Trust of all 10 Vehicles with respect to Percentage Recent Interactions (red color represents vehicle no. 1, magenta color represents vehicle no. 5, whereas green color represents vehicle no. 10. (Please note that the figure in the digital edition is displayed with color.)

Algorithm 5 Trust Computation TMF1 w.r.t. % Recent Interactions.

Require: Successful Interactions $s_{i,j,k}$, Unsuccessful Interactions $u_{i,j,k}$, Interaction Time Instant $k_{int_{i,j}}$, Previous Local Trust $LT_{i,j,k-1}$, Frequency of Interaction $\beta_{i,j,k}$, Distance $D_{i,j,k}$, Propagation Speed S_p, Neighbors N, Context $C_{txt_{i,j,k}}$

Ensure: Global Trust Percentage Interactions $GT_j k\%$

1: **for** $i \leftarrow 1$ to V **do**
2:     **for** $j \leftarrow 1$ to V **do**
3:         $DT_{i,j,k} \leftarrow Direct\ Trust(PDR_{i,j,k}, \Gamma_{i,j,k}, lemda_{i,j,k})$
4:         $IDT_{i,j,k} \leftarrow Indirect\ Trust(DT_{n,j,k}, \theta_{i,n,k})$
5:         $\beta_{i,j,k} \leftarrow Frequency\ of\ Interaction(x_{i,j,l})$
6:         $LT_{i,j,k} \leftarrow Local\ Trust(DT_{i,j,k}, \beta_{i,j,k}, IDT_{i,j,k})$
7:         $CDT_{i,j,k} \leftarrow Context\ Trust(PD_{i,j,k}, Co_{j,k}, F_{i,j,k})$
8:         $TLT_{j,k} \leftarrow Total\ Local\ Trust(LT_{i,j,k}, C_{txt_{i,j,k}}, CDT_{i,j,k})$
9:         $GT_{j,k} \leftarrow Global\ Trust(TLT_{i,j,k}, GT_{i,k-1})$
10:     **end for**
11: **end for**
12: **for** $k \leftarrow 0\%$ to 100% **do**
13:     $Threshold \leftarrow (1-k)^* RangeTime$
14:     **for** $i \leftarrow 1$ to V **do**
15:         **for** $j \leftarrow 1$ to V **do**
16:             **if** $k_{int_{i,j}} \geq Threshold$ **then**
17:                 $TLT_{i,j}k\% \leftarrow Agg(DT_{i,j,k}, IDT_{i,j,k}, CDT_{i,j,k})$
18:             **else**
19:                 $TLT_{i,j}k\% \leftarrow 0$
20:             **end if**
21:         **end for**
22:     **end for**
23:     $GT_j k\% \leftarrow Agg(TLT_{i,j}k\%, GT_{i,k-1})$
24: **end for**

---

interactions in the recent time windows influencing both, the direct and the indirect trusts. Similarly, vehicle no. 5 and 10 are also depicting an increase in their global trust values in the time windows of [0.5, 1] and [0.75, 1] as a result of improved direct and indirect trusts. The CDT for all vehicles in all time windows show very slight changes, this is because all the vehicles are communicating with their peers resulting in a highest possible familiarity and cooperation. The exact values for global trust and corresponding information regarding successful interactions, direct trust, indirect trust, and context dependent trust for selected vehicles (i.e., vehicle no. 3, 7, and 9) can be found in Tables 4.5, 4.6, 4.7, and 4.8, respectively.

Figure 4.5 illustrates the normalized DT, normalized PDR, and normalized forgetting factor (FF) for all 10 vehicles with respect to the recent 25% (illustrated in column 1), 50% (illustrated in column 2), 75% (illustrated in column 3), and 100% interactions (illustrated in column 4) among the nodes. PDR and FF are the two con-

Table 4.5
Global Trust Trend over Time.

Vehicle No.	25%	50%	75%	100%
1	0.9948	0.982	0.9607	0.9625
Neighbors	9	9	9	9
Successful Interactions	1132	2298	2956	3212
5	0.6862	0.6806	0.6550	0.6151
Neighbors	9	9	9	9
Successful Interactions	622	1125	1509	1659
10	0.6817	0.6754	0.6548	0.6329
Neighbors	9	9	9	9
Successful Interactions	721	1331	1808	1982

tributing parameters in the computation of DT. The normalized values for DT, PDR, and FF have been utilized to rescale the respective values on a scale of *0* to *1* for the sake of visibility. The depicted DT (illustrated in row 1) has been computed via Eq. 3.4, whereas the PDR, and FF (illustrated in row 2 and 3, respectively) have been calculated via Eqs. 3.1 and 3.3. The depicted parameters are composite parameters and have been computed via the same procedure mentioned above. The DT for vehicle no. 1 for the most recent time window, i.e., [7.5, 1] is the highest reflecting the lowest forgetting factor. The general trend of DT is identical to that of PDR, however, the values of DT are lower than the corresponding PDRs due to the introduction of forgetting factor. Similarly, the DT of vehicles 5 and 10 for the recent 25% interactions is higher than the recent 50%, 75%, and 100% interactions due to the decrease in forgetting factor most recently. Tables 4.6, 4.9, and 4.10 depict the DT, PDR, and FF for selected vehicles (i.e., vehicle no. 3, 7, and 9).

Figure 4.6 presents the normalized IDT, normalized neighbor trust (NT), and nor-

Table 4.6
Direct Trust Trend over Time.

Vehicle No.	25%	50%	75%	100%
1	1	0.9764	0.9441	0.9422
5	0.5937	0.5651	0.5166	0.4779
10	0.6056	0.5765	0.5334	0.5066

Table 4.7
Indirect Trust Trend over Time.

Vehicle No.	25%	50%	75%	100%
1	1	0.9774	0.9454	0.9459
5	0.5938	0.5663	0.5196	0.4812
10	0.5994	0.5696	0.5267	0.5025

malized confidence factor (CF) for all 10 vehicles with respect to the recent 25% (illustrated in column 1), 50% (illustrated in column 2), 75% (illustrated in column 3), and 100% interactions (illustrated in column 4) among the nodes. NT and CF are the two contributing parameters in the computation of IDT. The normalized values for IDT, NT, and CF have been utilized to rescale the respective values on a scale of 0 to 1 for the sake of visibility. The depicted IDT (illustrated in rows 1) has been computed via Eq. 3.6, whereas the NT, and CF (illustrated in rows 2, and 3, respectively) have been calculated by DT and via Eq. 3.5, respectively. The depicted parameters are composite parameters and have been computed via the same procedure mentioned above. The IDT for vehicle no. 1 for the most 25% recent interactions is the highest reflecting the highest neighbor trust. The general trend of IDT is similar to that of NT, however, the values of IDT are higher in some instances as compared to the corresponding NTs due to the impact of the confidence factor. Similarly, the IDT of vehicle 5 and 10 for the recent 25% interactions is higher than the recent 50%, 75%, and 100% interactions due to the increase in the neighbor trust most recently. Tables 4.7, 4.11, and 4.8 presents the IDT, NT, and CF for selected vehicles (i.e., vehicle no. 3, 7, and 9).

Figure 4.7 exhibits the normalized CDT, and normalized propagation delay (PD) for all 10 vehicles with respect to the recent 25% (illustrated in column 1), 50% (illustrated in column 2), 75% (illustrated in column 3), and 100% interactions (illustrated

Table 4.8
Context Dependent Trust Trend over Time.

Vehicle No.	25%	50%	75%	100%
1	0.9051	0.8992	0.9245	0.9237
5	0.9565	0.9747	0.9815	0.9717
10	0.9174	0.9172	0.9374	0.9359

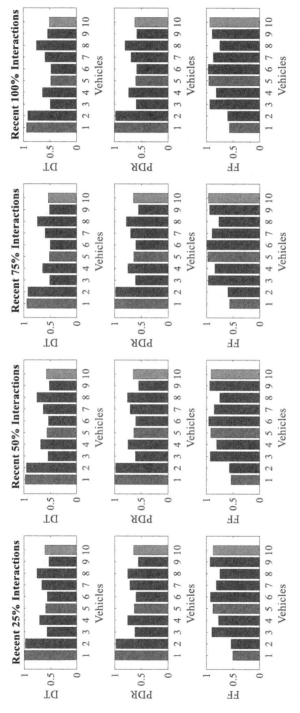

Figure 4.5 Time-varying Patterns for Direct Trust, Packet Delivery Ratio, and Forgetting Factor of all 10 Vehicles with respect to Percentage Recent Interactions (red color represents vehicle no. 1, magenta color represents vehicle no. 5, whereas green color represents vehicle no. 10). (Please note that the figure in the digital edition is displayed with color.)

Table 4.9

Packet Delivery Ratio Trend over Time.

Vehicle No.	25%	50%	75%	100%
1	0.9900	0.9978	1	0.9938
5	0.6277	0.6360	0.6404	0.6036
10	0.6392	0.6484	0.6474	0.6225

in column 4) among the nodes. PD is one of the three contributing parameters in the computation of CDT and is the only one shown in the figure as it influences the CDT scores the most based on our dataset. The normalized values for CDT, and PD have been utilized to rescale the respective values on a scale of *0* to *1* for the sake of visibility. The depicted CDT (illustrated in row 1) has been computed via Eq. 3.12, whereas the PD (illustrated in row 2) has been calculated via Eq. 3.9. The depicted parameters are composite parameters and have been computed via the same procedure mentioned above. The CDT for vehicle no. 1 for the most recent interactions is higher as compared to the 50% recent interactions whereas for the time windows [0.25, 1] the value rises before dropping again for 100% recent interactions demonstrating the influence of propagation delay. The trend of the CDT is a direct opposite to the variations in the propagation delay based on the distance among vehicles. The increase in the delay results in a drop in the CDT. Similarly, the CDT of vehicle 5 and 10 for the recent 75% interactions is the highest among all time windows owing to the lowest propagation delay and distance. Tables 4.8 and 4.13, provides the precise values for CDT, and PD for selected vehicles (i.e., vehicle no. 3, 7, and 9).

Safety-critical vehicular applications utilize instantaneous trust for decision making, whereas non-safety vehicular applications make decisions by relying on over time trust patterns. Accordingly, Figure 4.8 delineates the time-varying global trust patterns of three vehicles. Figure 4.8(a) depicts the patterns of vehicle no. 1 and it

Table 4.10

Forgetting Factor Trend over Time.

Vehicle No.	25%	50%	75%	100%
1	0.5032	0.5361	0.5648	0.5668
5	0.8777	0.9185	0.9761	0.9537
10	0.8724	0.9130	0.9628	0.9341

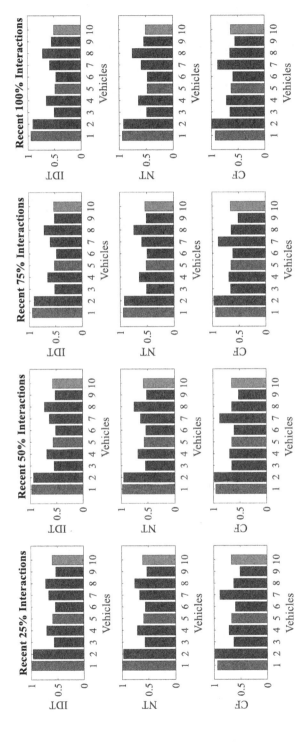

Figure 4.6 Time-varying Patterns for Indirect Trust, Neighbor Trust, and Confidence Factor of all 10 Vehicles with respect to Percentage Recent Interactions (red color represents vehicle no. 1, magenta color represents vehicle no. 5, whereas green color represents vehicle no. 10). (Please note that the figure in the digital edition is displayed with color.)

Table 4.11
Neighbor Trust Trend over Time.

Vehicle No.	25%	50%	75%	100%
1	1	0.9764	0.9441	0.9422
5	0.5937	0.5651	0.5166	0.4779
10	0.6056	0.5765	0.5334	0.5066

can be observed that global trust resulting from aggregating the most recent inter-actions (i.e., 25%) and for 50% recent interactions for this vehicle is slightly higher as compared to the other time windows. Therefore, this vehicle is trustworthy when it comes to safety-critical vehicular applications. Moreover, the vehicle maintains a stable behavior over time, i.e., there are no sudden drops in the global trust indicating that the said vehicle may also be reliable for non-safety vehicular applications. Similarly, Figure 4.8(b) presents the patterns of vehicle no. 7 and it can be observed that the trust aggregating the most recent interactions (i.e., 25%) of this vehicle is the highest making this vehicle reliable for safety-critical vehicular applications. In addition, the said vehicle demonstrates a rather stable and slightly increasing trend over time making it reliable for non-safety vehicular applications as well. Furthermore, Figure 4.8(c) illustrates the behavioral patterns of vehicle no. 9 and it can be seen that the said vehicle also has a stable trust score over time, however, the trust scores are slightly decreasing and then rising which can be an indication of a selfish behavior. Though, the drop in the values is not significant enough to cause concern of a selfish conduct. Therefore, this vehicle is suitable for both safety and non-safety vehicular applications.

4.4.3 COMPARISON - TMF1 AND TMF2

As discussed in detail in Chapter 3 - Section 3.3 (System Model for TMF1) and Chapter 4 - Section 4.3 (System Model for TMF2), both trust management models employ different datasets, i.e., TMF1 utilizes the dataset generated by a java simulator, whereas TMF2 makes use of a real IoT dataset from CRAWDAD. Owing to the unique characteristics captured in each of the datasets, the extracted trust parameters also vary. Consequently, the formulation of the final trust scores for each trust management model (i.e., TMF1 and TMF2) is different based on the varying trust parameters. This demonstrates that a generic trust management framework can not be applied for every scenario, instead the trust management systems are highly dependant on the available communication information. The simulation results discussed in Sections 4.4.1 and 4.4.2 depict that studying the time varying behavior can aid in understanding the suitable applications, i.e., safety-critical and non-safety vehicular applications, for each individual vehicle regardless of the dataset, trust parameters,

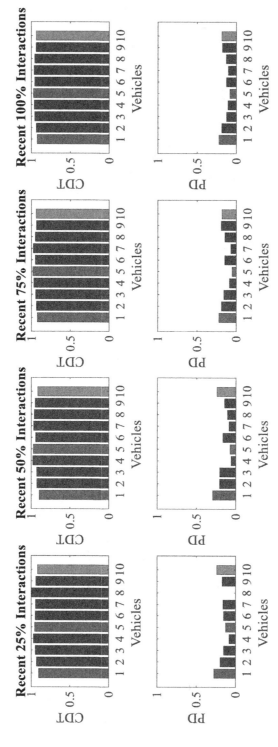

Figure 4.7 Time-varying Patterns for Context Dependent Trust, and Propagation Delay of all 10 Vehicles with respect to Percentage Recent Interactions (red color represents vehicle no. 1, magenta color represents vehicle no. 5, whereas green color represents vehicle no. 10). (Please note that the figure in the digital edition is displayed with color.)

Table 4.12
Confidence Factor Trend over Time.

Vehicle No.	25%	50%	75%	100%
1	0.9401	0.9578	0.9457	0.9301
5	0.6699	0.6497	0.6519	0.6308
10	0.6723	0.6507	0.6571	0.6360

Table 4.13
Propagation Delay Trend over Time.

Vehicle No.	25%	50%	75%	100%
1	0.7230	0.7056	0.7796	0.7771
5	0.8730	0.9262	0.9461	0.9174
10	0.7588	0.7582	0.8173	0.8127

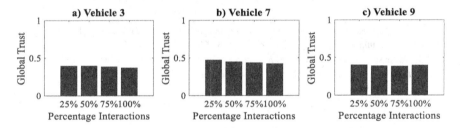

Figure 4.8 Global Trust Variation over Time for a) Vehicle no. 3, b) Vehicle no. 7, and c) Vehicle no. 9. (Please note that the figure in the digital edition is displayed with color.)

and the formulation of final trust scores. For both trust management models, i.e., TMF1 and TMF2 discussed in this chapter, the simulation tool used to implement the said models is the same, i.e., MATLAB.

4.5 CHAPTER SUMMARY

Exchanging safety-critical data among vehicles requires high level of security and trustworthiness. The trust related attributes of current trust management models are often assigned manually with certain weights without the consideration of the dynamic Internet of Vehicles. In this chapter, a time-aware trust management model has been proposed that addresses the quantification of weights (in the form of timeliness and interaction frequency) associated with the contributing parameters (e.g., familiarity and packet delivery ratio) and the quantification of trust by quantifying the said contributing parameters as well as their weights utilizing a real IoT dataset. Moreover, the impact of weights on each parameter along with the influence of individual parameters on the final trust (i.e., aggregated trust for TMF2 and global trust for TMF1) score has been discussed for the trust evaluation framework proposed in this chapter (i.e., TMF2) and the one envisaged in Chapter 3 (i.e., TMF1). Furthermore, our analysis reflects the time-based analysis of the vehicles' trust which facilitates studying the behavioral patterns of individual vehicles and further investigates the trust-based patterns for safety-critical and non-safety vehicular applications.

It would be educative to investigate the effectiveness of other computational techniques towards formulating a trust management model, and more importantly, identifying misbehaving entities without having to pre-define or quantify the minimum acceptable trust threshold. Accordingly, in the next chapter, we would like to broaden our horizon and introduce machine learning techniques while utilizing an almost similar set of trust parameters along with a self-learning threshold for dishonest vehicle classification.

REFERENCES

1. N. B. Truong, T.-W. Um, B. Zhou, and G. M. Lee. *From Personal Experience to Global Reputation for Trust Evaluation in the Social Internet of Things*. In *2017 IEEE Global Communications Conference (GLOBECOM)*, pp. 1–7 (IEEE, 2017).
2. O. Samuel, N. Javaid, A. Khalid, M. Imrarn, and N. Nasser. *A Trust Management System for Multi-agent System in Smart Grids using Blockchain Technology*. In *2020 IEEE Global Communications Conference (GLOBECOM)*, pp. 1–6 (2020).
3. A. Alnasser and H. Sun. *Global Roaming Trust-based Model for V2X Communications*. In *IEEE Conference on Computer Communications Workshops (INFOCOM WKSHPS)*, pp. 1–6 (2019).
4. A. Mahmood, B. Butler, W. E. Zhang, Q. Z. Sheng, and S. A. Siddiqui. *A Hybrid Trust Management Heuristic for VANETs*. In *2019 IEEE International Conference on Pervasive Computing and Communications Workshops (PerCom Workshops)*, pp. 748–752 (2019).
5. P. Dass, S. Misra, and C. Roy. *T-Safe: Trustworthy Service Provisioning for IoT-based Intelligent Transport Systems*. IEEE Transactions on Vehicular Technology 69(9), 9509 (2020).
6. N. A. Heckert, J. J. Filliben, C. M. Croarkin, B. Hembree, W. F. Guthrie, P. Tobias, J. Prinz, et al. *Handbook 151: NIST/SEMATECH e-Handbook of Statistical Methods* (2002).
7. J. Zheng and M. Huang. *Traffic Flow Forecast through Time Series Analysis based on Deep Learning*. IEEE Access 8, 82562 (2020).
8. Q. Wu, H. Ge, P. Fan, J. Wang, Q. Fan, and Z. Li. *Time-dependent Performance Analysis of the 802.11p-based Platooning Communications Under Disturbance*. IEEE Transactions on Vehicular Technology 69(12), 15760 (2020).
9. H. Gao, C. Liu, Y. Yin, Y. Xu, and Y. Li. *A Hybrid Approach to Trust Node Assessment and Management for VANETs Cooperative Data Communication: Historical Interaction Perspective*. IEEE Transactions on Intelligent Transportation Systems pp. 1–10 (2021).

10. X. Chen, J. Ding, and Z. Lu. *A Decentralized Trust Management System for Intelligent Transportation Environments.* IEEE Transactions on Intelligent Transportation Systems 23(1), 558 (2020).

11. H. Zhang, J. Liu, H. Zhao, P. Wang, and N. Kato. *Blockchain-based Trust Management for Internet of Vehicles.* IEEE Transactions on Emerging Topics in Computing 9(3), 1397 (2021).

12. F. Ahmad, F. Kurugollu, C. A. Kerrache, S. Sezer, and L. Liu. *NOTRINO: A NOvel Hybrid Trust Management Scheme for Internet-of-Vehicles.* IEEE Transactions on Vehicular Technology 70(9), 9244 (2021).

13. H. Xia, S.-s. Zhang, Y. Li, Z.-k. Pan, X. Peng, and X.-z. Cheng. *An Attack-Resistant Trust Inference Model for Securing Routing in Vehicular Ad Hoc Networks.* IEEE Transactions on Vehicular Technology 68(7), 7108 (2019).

14. J. Zhang, K. Zheng, D. Zhang, and B. Yan. *AATMS: An Anti-Attack Trust Management Scheme in VANET.* IEEE Access 8, 21077 (2020).

15. X. Huang, R. Yu, J. Kang, and Y. Zhang. *Distributed Reputation Management for Secure and Efficient Vehicular Edge Computing and Networks.* IEEE Access 5, 25408 (2017).

16. A. V. Leonov and G. A. Litvinov. *Simulation-based Packet Delivery Performance Evaluation with Different Parameters in Flying Ad Hoc Network (FANET) using AODV and OLSR.* In *Journal of Physics: Conference Series*, vol. 1015, p. 032178 (IOP Publishing, 2018).

5 Machine Learning based Trust Management for the Internet of Vehicles

This chapter focuses on employing machine learning techniques to cope with the weight and misbehavior detection threshold quantification in IoV. It utilizes a real IoT communication dataset by transforming it into an IoV format and computes the feature matrix for four parameters, i.e., packet delivery ratio, familiarity, timeliness, and interaction frequency, in two different ways: (a) all of the stated parameters computed by each trustor for a trustee are treated as individual features, and (b) mean of each single parameter computed by all of the trustors for a trustee is regarded as a collective feature. Different machine learning algorithms were employed for classifying vehicles as *trustworthy* and *untrustworthy*. Simulation results revealed that the classification via mean parametric scores yielded more accurate results in contrast to the one which takes into account the parametric score of each trustor for a trustee on individual basis.

5.1 OVERVIEW

As previously explained, the state-of-the-art technological breakthroughs in IoV over the past few decades have played a significant role in the advancement of Intelligent Transportation Systems (ITS) which is an indispensable constituent of the emerging and promising paradigm of smart cities [1]. Machine learning, a prominent flavor of artificial intelligence, is one of the most effective and powerful tool to develop systems in an adaptive and predictive manner, has been widely employed in traditional wireless and vehicular networks. Vehicular networks are highly dynamic in nature and so, the data-driven techniques aid machine learning to tackle the challenges experienced by traditional solutions for these ever-changing networks [2].

Machine learning has been extensively and effectively applied in various domains, e.g., healthcare, robotics, transportation, computer vision, and it primarily focuses on developing systems with intelligence to be able to work in complex environments. It relies on identifying patterns and inherent structures by analyzing large volumes of data. Being a data-centric methodology, definite suppositions/assumptions have not been imposed on the dissemination of data which provides resilience to process miscellaneous data originated from diverse sources. In vehicular networks, it offers a variety of tools to utilize and help acquire data from heterogeneous sources enabling the system to take well-informed decisions and deliver services, e.g., traffic control and forecasting, in addition to mitigating issues related to communication. Machine learning algorithms are categorized as unsupervised learning algorithms, supervised learning algorithms, and reinforcement learning algorithms. The process usually involves two phases, 1) training phase, wherein training data is utilized to train the specific algorithm in order to generate output, and 2) testing phase, wherein the testing data is used with the trained model to yield results.

Supervised learning requires a dataset with labels or ground truth representing different classes of data. These labels can be either continuous (i.e., for classification) or discrete (i.e., for regression). Subsequently, a part of this data is utilized for training purposes and the other part for classification or regression testing. The objective of this type of learning is to map out the decision space from the input feature space, in other words, it estimates the mapping function so that it can be applied to any future data in order to generate results. The larger the volume of the data, the more the more accurate the mapping function gets. On the contrary, unsupervised learning makes use of data without labels or ground truth. It is often not possible to acquire a large volume of labelled data in certain domains and unsupervised learning helps with describing data samples effectively in such datasets by identifying underlying variables and/or structures by employing Bayesian inference. Clustering is one of the most common variants of unsupervised learning, wherein multiple data samples are grouped together based on the similarities in their features and each group is termed as a cluster [3].

As mentioned earlier in Chapter 3 and 4, while accumulating trust values, it is indispensable to allocate effective weights to the influencing parameters to reflect their reasonable impact in order to generate accurate and intuitive trust values, however, the quantification of these weights poses a considerable challenge. This essentially necessitates an in-depth knowledge of the effects of each of these individual influential parameters on the trust evaluation (i.e., corresponding to divergent traffic scenarios and vehicular applications) and is a complex analysis problem in its own essence. Subsequent to trust evaluation, an optimal threshold selection for misbehavior detection is of huge significance, as if the threshold is too low, the system will not be able to filter out all the dishonest nodes, whereas, if the said threshold is set too high, the trustworthy nodes might also get evicted from the network. Accordingly, this chapter primarily focuses on:

- Assessing the dataset (i.e., CRAWDAD dataset[1]) to formulate effective trust parameters, i.e., *packet delivery ratio* – delineating the throughput between the trustor and the trustee, *familiarity* – depicting how good the trustor knows the trustee, *timeliness* – manifesting the freshness of the interaction among a trustor ans a trustee, and *interaction frequency* – defining how frequently the trustor and the trustee interacted with one another;
- Exploiting machine learning techniques (i.e., support vector machine (SVM), k-nearest neighbors (KNN), ensemble subspace KNN, and subspace discriminant) to cope with the problem of effective weights assignment and optimal threshold selection in vehicular networks;

---

[1]https://ieee-dataport.org/open-access/crawdad-thlabsigcomm2009

- Computing the feature matrix in two different ways (a) all of the stated parameters computed by each trustor for a trustee are treated as individual features and (b) the mean of each single parameter computed by all of the trustors for a trustee is regarded as a collective feature.

It thus employs a real IoT dataset (i.e., the same dataset utilized in Chapter 4) by transforming it into an IoV format and subsequently computes the feature matrix for four parameters. Subsequent to the feature extraction and labelling process, different machine learning algorithms, i.e., support vector machine (SVM), k-nearest neighbors (KNN), ensemble subspace KNN, and subspace discriminant were employed so as to classify vehicles into two classes, i.e., *trustworthy* and *untrustworthy*. Simulation results revealed that the classification via mean parametric scores yielded more accurate results in contrast to the one that takes into account the parametric score of each trustor for a trustee on individual basis.

5.1.1 ORGANIZATION OF THE CHAPTER

The remainder of this chapter is organized as follows. Section 5.2 illustrates the existing state of the art specific to this chapter only in the said domain, Section 5.3 delineates the envisaged system model, Section 5.4 discusses the simulation results, whereas, Section 5.5 concludes the chapter.

5.2 RELATED WORK

It is pertinent to note that this related work is specific to this chapter only. A brief glimpse of the literature reveals a number of research studies envisaging various trust management models and intrusion detection frameworks for identifying malicious vehicles and subsequently eliminating them from within the network. In [4], a trust management model based on job marketing signaling scheme has been proposed in order to promote cooperative behavior amongst different vehicles in a network. A credit is assigned to each individual node within the network, and every time a node behaves maliciously, an amount depending on the cost of the attack is deducted from the originally allocated credit as to discourage the malicious vehicles. Similarly, once a node manifests a positive participation, the credit is subsequently increased to encourage the node's participation and its cooperation with other nodes in the network.

In [5], the authors proposed a fuzzy logic based decentralized trust management framework that flags the unintentional misbehavior of a target vehicle by combining the trustor's own experience and the suggested evaluation of it's neighbors. Moreover, indirect trust was also evaluated for trustees which were not directly connected to the trustor by utilizing the notion of reinforcement learning.

A blockchain-based privacy preserving distributed trust management scheme has been proposed in [6] which breaks the linkability between the public key and vehicle's real identity to achieve the anonymity when the certification authority issues or revokes the respective certificates. All the messages were stored in the blockchain and trust scores were assigned to each individual vehicle by evaluating the data transmitted by them thereby discouraging misconduct. To mitigate the adversarial effects of malicious attacks and misbehaving vehicles in Vehicular networks, a noteworthy solution is to introduce an intrusion detection system (IDS) which utilizes signature- and anomaly-based detection schemes for the said purpose. A decentralized cooperative IDS has been proposed in [7] which employed privacy-preserving distributed machine learning for ensuring a private collaboration. The collaborative nature of the proposed scheme encourages all the vehicles within the network to share their trained data along with the ground truth to provide a scalable, cost-efficacious, and higher quality mechanism. Moreover, a distributed classification solution has also been achieved using ADMM (i.e., alternating direction method of multipliers) algorithm. The IDS suggested in [8] inspects traffic, employs a deep belief network for simplifying the data dimensionality, and distinguishes genuine service requests from the counterfeited ones. Furthermore, it implements a service-specific clustering to ensure that the cloud services are available continuously thereby guaranteeing both the quality-of-service and quality-of-experience. In [9], the IDS amalgamated support vector machine and the promiscuous mode in order to build the trust table for the identification and prevention of attacks, wherein every vehicle monitors its neighbor for the misconduct. Similarly, authors in [10] introduced multiple types of attacks in the proposed scheme by altering the safety messages exchanged by vehicles and subsequently classified different malicious (active) attacks by extracting distinguishing features and via utilizing machine learning techniques.

Whilst the existing literature has already demonstrated some significant contributions by applying numerous machine learning techniques, nevertheless, they still lack the potential of being a generic algorithm that could be commonly applied to any service domain and across diverse parameters. Moreover, the existing research studies only rely on the conventional factors in the trust assessment process and the impact of the influential parameters (i.e., packet delivery ratio, familiarity, timeliness, and interaction frequency) on the trust assessment and aggregation process has been completely ignored.

5.3   SYSTEM MODEL

We hereby propose a machine learning based trust management scheme to identify malicious (dishonest) vehicles for eradicating them from the network in order to restrict them to cause any further harm and to conserve precious network resources. The proposed system model comprises of two main steps. The first step utilizes unsupervised learning algorithms to cluster and label the data, whereas, the second step relies on supervised learning algorithms for classifying the vehicles into two groups, i.e., *untrustworthy* and *trustworthy* as mentioned in Table 5.1.

The simulations are performed for a vehicular network (or a cluster) comprising of N vehicles. Every vehicle i, wherein $i = 1, \ldots, N$ has j one-hop neighbors, wherein $j = 1, \ldots, N$ and $(i \neq j)$, and evaluates them, i.e., i is the trustor and j is the trustee. The evaluation transpires on the basis of four parameters – packet delivery

Table 5.1
Classification Groups.

Groups	Labels
1	Untrustworthy
2	Trustworthy

ratio ($PDR_{i,j}$), familiarity ($FMR_{i,j}$), timeliness ($TML_{i,j}$), and interaction frequency ($IFR_{i,j}$). The parameter values vary in the range of 0 and 1, wherein 0 represents the lowest correlation between a pair of a trustor and a trustee, whereas, 1 signifies the highest correlation of the said pair. Table 5.2 outlines the mathematical notations employed in the system model.

Table 5.2
Notations & Definitions.

Notation	Definition
N	Total number of vehicles
i	Trustor
j	Trustee
$PDR_{i,j}$	Packet Delivery Ratio among a pair of a *Trustor* and a *Trustee*
$FMR_{i,j}$	Familiarity among a pair of a *Trustor* and a *Trustee*
$TML_{i,j}$	Timeliness of the interaction among a *Trustee* and a *Trustor*
$IFR_{i,j}$	Interaction frequency among a *Trustee* and a *Trustor*
$M_{i,j}$	Successful message transmission from a *Trustee* to a *Trustor*
M_{i_j}	Total number of messages sent from a *Trustee* to a *Trustor*
$F_{i,j}$	Common friends among a *Trustee* and a *Trustor*
F_i	Total number of friends of a *Trustor*
$T_{i,j}$	Time instance when the interaction took place
$T_{current}$	Current time instance
$I_{i,j}$	Interaction among a pair of a *Trustor* and a *Trustee*
I_i	Total number of interactions of a *Trustor*
$FM1$	Feature Matrix 1
PDR_{avg_j}	Average packet delivery ratio of a *Trustee*
FMR_{avg_j}	Average familiarity of a *Trustee*
TML_{avg_j}	Average timeliness of a *Trustee*
IFR_{avg_j}	Average interaction frequency of a *Trustee*
$FM2$	Feature Matrix 2

5.3.1   DATASET & FEATURE EXTRACTION

For the proposed system model, we have used an IoT dataset from CRAWDAD[1] by suitably transforming it into an IoV format. The proposed trust management model has been evaluated using MATLAB simulations for all 76 vehicles. We defined four scoring parameters, i.e., packet delivery ratio, familiarity, timeliness and interaction frequency for evaluating each node in the network.

Packet Delivery Ratio ($PDR_{i,j}$)**:** The packet delivery ratio $(0 \leq PDR_{i,j} \leq 1)$ is the degree of how well a trustor is connected to the trustee. In other words, the packet delivery ratio represents the proportion of the messages received by a trustor and is computed via Eq. 5.1 as:

$$PDR_{i,j} = \frac{M_{i,j}}{M_{i_j}} \tag{5.1}$$

where, $M_{i,j}$ is the number of messages sent by the trustee j that were successfully received by the trustor i, and M_{i_j} is the total number of messages sent to i by j.

Familiarity ($FMR_{i,j}$)**:** Familiarity $(0 \leq FMR_{i,j} \leq 1)$ refers to the degree of how well a trustor knows the trustee. The familiarity is computed via Eq. 5.2 as:

$$FMR_{i,j} = \frac{F_{i,j}}{F_i} \tag{5.2}$$

where, $F_{i,j}$ is the number of common friends between both the trustor and the trustee, and F_i is the total number of the trustor's friends.

Timeliness ($TML_{i,j}$)**:** Timeliness $(0 \leq TML_{i,j} \leq 1)$ refers to the degree of how fresh the interaction among a trustor and a trustee is. The timeliness is computed via Eq. 5.3 as:

$$TML_{i,j} = \frac{T_{i,j}}{T_{current}} \tag{5.3}$$

where, $T_{i,j}$ is the time when the interaction among the trustor and the trustee took place, and $T_{current}$ is the current time instance.

Interaction Frequency ($IFR_{i,j}$)**:** Interaction Frequency $(0 \leq IFR_{i,j} \leq 1)$ refers to the degree of how often a trustor interacts with the trustee. The interaction frequency is computed via Eq. 5.4 as:

$$IFR_{i,j} = \frac{\sum I_{i,j}}{\sum I_i} \tag{5.4}$$

where, $I_{i,j}$ is the interaction between a trustor and a trustee, and I_i is the total number of the trustor's interactions.

These four parameters are calculated for each pair of a trustor and a trustee that exists in the vehicular network and the scores are recorded in two different feature matrices. In the first feature matrix, the rows represent the trustees (there are $n=76$

---

[1]https://ieee-dataport.org/open-access/crawdad-thlabsigcomm2009

number of rows) and the columns represent the said parameters (PDR, FMR, TML, and IFR) ascertained by each trustor for each trustee on an indiviudal basis, i.e., there are $4N - 4$ number of columns. This feature matrix (see Eq. 5.5) is formed with an intent to inspect the impact of each trustor for a trustee against each parameter in the final classification.

$$FM1 = \begin{bmatrix} PDR_{11} \ldots PDR_{1N-1} & FMR_{11} \ldots FMR_{1N-1} & TML_{11} \ldots TML_{1N-1} & IFR_{11} \ldots IFR_{1N-1} \\ \vdots \ddots \vdots & \vdots \ddots \vdots & \vdots \ddots \vdots & \vdots \ddots \vdots \\ PDR_{N1} \ldots PDR_{NN-1} & FMR_{N1} \ldots FMR_{NN-1} & TML_{N1} \ldots TML_{NN-1} & IFR_{N1} \ldots IFR_{NN-1} \end{bmatrix} \quad (5.5)$$

In the second feature matrix, the rows represent the trustees, i.e., there are $n = 76$ number of rows and the columns represent the mean of each parameter (PDR, FMR, TML, and IFR) computed for each trustee by all the trustors, i.e., there are 4 columns in total. The means for PDR, FMR, TML, and IFR are obtained via Eqs. 5.6, 5.7, 5.8, and 5.9, respectively. This feature matrix (see Eq. 5.10) is formed with an intent to classify the vehicles on the basis of their mean parametric scores.

$$PDR_{avg_j} = \frac{\sum_{i=1}^{N} PDR_{i,j}}{N-1}, \, i \neq j \quad (5.6)$$

$$FMR_{avg_j} = \frac{\sum_{i=1}^{N} FMR_{i,j}}{N-1}, \, i \neq j \quad (5.7)$$

$$TML_{avg_j} = \frac{\sum_{i=1}^{N} TML_{i,j}}{N-1}, \, i \neq j \quad (5.8)$$

$$IFR_{avg_j} = \frac{\sum_{i=1}^{N} IFR_{i,j}}{N-1}, \, i \neq j \quad (5.9)$$

where, $PDR_{i,j}$, $FMR_{i,j}$, $TML_{i,j}$, and $IFR_{i,j}$ is the computed packet delivery ratio, familiarity, timeliness, and interaction frequency, respectively, among a pair of a trustor i and a trustee j.

$$FM2 = \begin{bmatrix} PDR_{avg_1} & FMR_{avg_1} & TML_{avg_1} & IFR_{avg_1} \\ \vdots & \vdots & \vdots & \vdots \\ PDR_{avg_N} & FMR_{avg_N} & TML_{avg_N} & IFR_{avg_N} \end{bmatrix} \quad (5.10)$$

5.3.2 CLUSTERING & LABELING

The computed score for each parameter (i.e., via Eq. 5.1–5.4) is used to classify the vehicles into two clusters, i.e., *trustworthy* and *untrustworthy*. The said clusters are ascertained by employing the algorithms that we have envisaged on the basis of un-supervised learning algorithms, i.e., *k-means, fuzzy c-means, hierarchical clustering*, and *gaussian mixture*, to label the feature matrices obtained in the previous subsec-tion. The key rationale for employing all of the four unsupervised learning algorithms is to ensure a credible, reliable and persistent ground truth.

K-means clustering is a partitional method, i.e., it assumes that expressing a given dataset in the form of finite groups, known as clusters, having individual selection criteria is achievable. Each group has a group profile, known as the cluster prototype that defines the data points inside that particular group. Partitioning methods rely on the difference or distance among a data point and a group's prototype. K-means algorithms are recognized as the most well-known and earliest partitional method [11]. Initialization parameters influence these algorithms in addition to assigning a priori to these clusters [12, 13, 14]. K-means clustering converges fast due to its simplicity [15].

Fuzzy c-means clustering relies on euclidean distance among the data points and the centroids. Similar to k-means, fuzzy c-means clustering is also impacted by the initialization parameters, however, they achieve convergence more rapidly as com-pared to k-means clustering. Due to the symmetric nature of euclidean distance, its reliance on the euclidean distance implies that the significance of variables in a given dataset is considered to be the same. In this particular clustering algorithm, each data point may belong to multiple groups, therefore, it is know as a soft clustering method, wherein a probability or likelihood is associated with each data point to be a part of a certain group or cluster [16, 17].

Hierarchical clustering employs a bottom-up (i.e., agglomerative) approach or a top-down (i.e., divisive) technique to group data points into hierarchical groups or clusters. It is widely applied to analyze data statistically and for data mining. In this clustering method, it is not a requirement to initiate the number of resulting clusters, however, its computational efficiency is quite high and such methods are not suitable for high dimensional datasets. Hierarchical clustering differs from the aforementioned partitional methods as they generate a hierarchical breakdown of data instead of separating it into multiple groups depending on the prototype [18].

Gaussian mixture is a soft clustering method, i.e., it assigns probabilities or like-lihood to each data point to be classified in a specific cluster. It takes preference over k-means as it takes into consideration the variation in the data which refers to the shape of the curve, therefore, is appropriate for elliptical shaped clusters as well as the circular ones. Gaussian mixture models employed for clustering suppose that ev-ery data point forms a Gaussian distribution. This clustering technique is believed to outperform other clustering algorithms as it factors in the number of clusters and the position of the same along with the shape [19, 20, 21].

The cluster close to the origin is categorized as *malicious*, whereas, the other is regarded as the *trusted* one. In other words, the vehicles having a high parametric value are more credible in contrast to the ones having a lower parametric value. The obtained labels are subsequently incorporated into the feature matrices. It is worth noting that both of the feature matrices will have different labels as the data points inside the said matrices are in contrast with one another. Algorithm 6 depicts clustering and labeling via fuzzy c-means, where the data points in the obtained feature matrices are classified into two clusters and labels are assigned to each data point according to their distance from the origin.

Algorithm 6 Labeling using Fuzzy C-means.

Input: FM1/FM2

Output: Labels

1: Initialize cluster centers $c_1, c_2, ..., c_j$

2: **for** $j = 1\,to\,2$ **do**

3:     Repeat until convergence:

4:     Calculate the membership values w_{ij}

5:     $w_{ij} \leftarrow \dfrac{1}{\frac{||X^{(i)}-c_j||}{||X^{(i)}-c_k||}}$

6:     **for** $i = 1\,to\,n$ **do**

7:         $a^{(i)} \leftarrow arg\,min_c\,w_{ij}^m\,||X^{(i)} - c_j||^2$

8:     **end for**

9:     $K^{(j)}(a,c) \leftarrow arg\,min_j\,K(a,c)$

10: **end for**

11: **for** $i = 1\,to\,n$ **do**

12:     **if** $a^{(i)}$ close to *origin* **then**

13:         $Labels^{(i)} \leftarrow 1$

14:     **else**

15:         $Labels^{(i)} \leftarrow 2$

16:     **end if**

17: **end for**

5.3.3 CLASSIFICATION MODEL

Subsequent to the clustering and labelling process, the supervised learning classifiers have been employed to the resulting feature matrices for training with a *5-fold cross validation* so as to identify malicious vehicles by obtaining the decision boundary due to their distinct characteristics. A variety of machine learning techniques based on *k-nearest neighbors, support vector machine*, and *ensemble classification models* have been utilized.

K-nearest neighbors (KNN) algorithm is considered as one of the simplest techniques and is employed for both regression and classification. It employs the notion of neighborhood proximity, i.e., similarity or distance-based measure is utilized for classification. This means that every new data point is categorized as a part of the same class as that of the nearest neighbor,i.e., the closest data item. The primary goal of this algorithm is to generate a prediction model relying on the training data points and to predict relevant labels for the testing data points. Despite the ease of use, KNN is not suitable for certain applications as it caches the entire set of data points in the memory, and is computationally complex and costly [22, 23].

Support vector machine (SVM) is a well-known technique and can also be used for both classification and regression. It yields highly accurate results, however, it is more suitable for small datasets due to longer processing times. It works by determining an optimum boundary for data separation relying on the labels, i.e., the ground truth, assigned to these data points. SVM is less susceptible to overfitting, wherein the model fits exactly or too close to a part of the dataset, i.e., a small collection of data points. It is capable of supporting high-dimensional data and can be used for linear as well as non-linear classification of data. Among multiple decision boundaries, SVM formulates the one with a maximum distance from the data points in the training dataset belonging to any of the classes. The greater the distance, the higher the accuracy and the lower the classification error are [22, 24].

Ensemble classification models are generally formulated by combining multiple base classifiers, wherein each classifier individually determines the decision boundaries between different classes by learning patterns from the training data. The classification outcome of these classifiers on the testing data is generated by the amalgamation of separate decisions of each of the base classifiers. The results yielded by these ensemble classifiers are more accurate in comparison to the individual base classifiers given that the individual errors of the contributing base classifiers are uncorrelated. The modern techniques to devise ensembles utilize distinct portions of the entire training set to train individual base classifiers resulting in uncorrelated errors. The classification outcome individual base classifiers are consolidated to produce the final decision by employing majority voting or algebraic combiners depending on the form of decisions, i.e., discrete or continuous, respectively [25, 26, 27].

Algorithm 7 delineates the classification and decision boundary for the data points from the computed feature matrices by utilizing a variety of classification algorithms with a 5 fold validation.

Algorithm 7 Classification & Decision Boundary.

    Input: FM1/FM2, Labels
    Output: Accuracy, Decision boundary
1: Initiate n classification models with k fold validation ($k = 5$)
2: **for** $z = 1\,to\,n$ **do**
3:    Find the classification accuracy and decision boundary of each machine learning model
4:    $[Acc_z, B_z] = model_z(FM1/FM2, Labels, k)$
5: **end for**

5.4 SIMULATION RESULTS

This section focuses on the simulation results yielded by applying the envisaged trust model on the dataset employing MATLAB.

5.4.1 CLUSTERING & LABELING

It is pertinent to mentions that only the clustering of data points employing fuzzy c-means are illustrated in figures. The clustering of data points (i.e., vehicles) from *FM1* is presented in Figs. 5.1 – 5.6 only for vehicles 1–6 whereas the clustering of

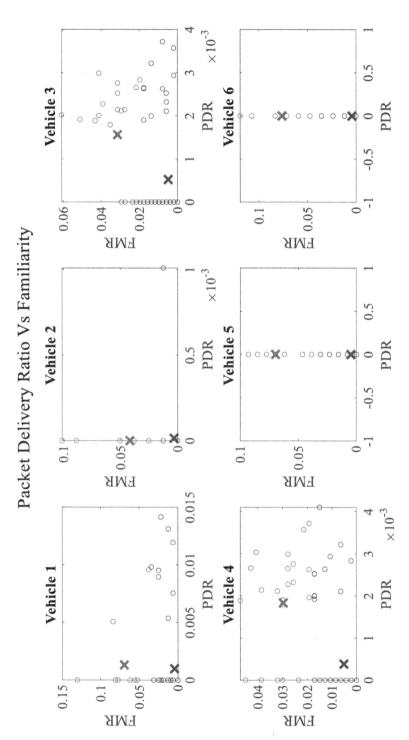

Figure 5.1 Clustering for Labels using Unsupervised Learning for Packet Delivery Ratio vs. Familiarity for vehicles 1 – 6 (The cluster in blue represents *untrustworthy* vehicles whereas the cluster in red depicts *trustworthy* vehicles). (Please note that the figure in the digital edition is displayed

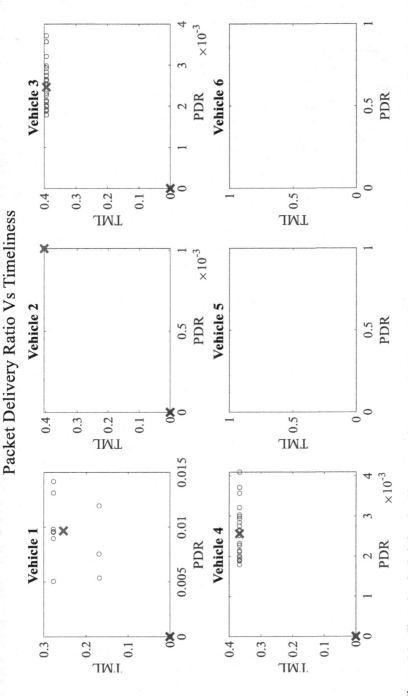

Figure 5.2 Clustering for Labels using Unsupervised Learning for Packet Delivery Ratio vs. Timeliness for vehicles 1 – 6 (The cluster in blue represents *untrustworthy* vehicles whereas the cluster in red depicts *trustworthy* vehicles). (Please note that the figure in the digital edition is displayed with color.)

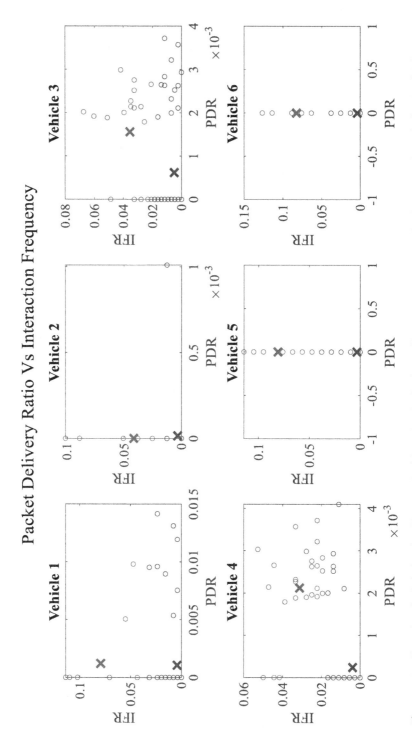

Figure 5.3 Clustering for Labels using Unsupervised Learning for Packet Delivery Ratio vs. Interaction Frequency for vehicles 1 – 6 (The cluster in blue represents *untrustworthy* vehicles whereas the cluster in red depicts *trustworthy* vehicles). (Please note that the figure in the digital edition is

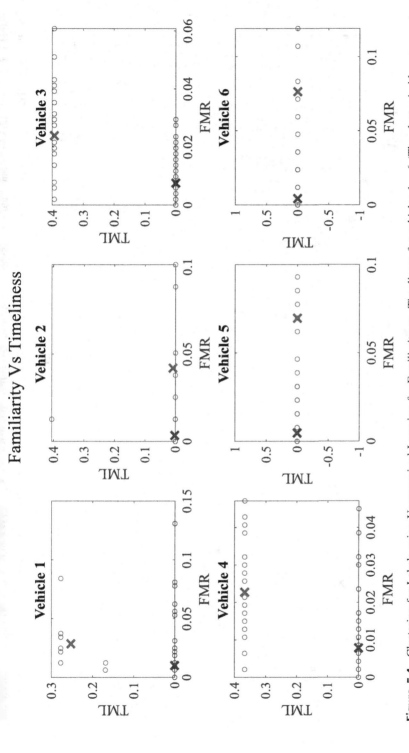

Figure 5.4 Clustering for Labels using Unsupervised Learning for Familiarity *vs.* Timeliness for vehicles 1 – 6 (The cluster in blue represents *untrustworthy* vehicles whereas the cluster in red depicts *trustworthy* vehicles). (Please note that the figure in the digital edition is displayed with color.)

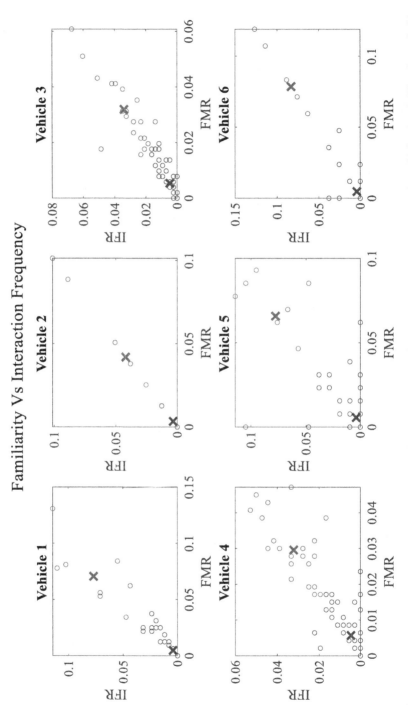

Figure 5.5 Clustering for Labels using Unsupervised Learning for Familiarity *vs.* Interaction Frequency for vehicles 1 – 6 (The cluster in blue represents *untrustworthy* vehicles whereas the cluster in red depicts *trustworthy* vehicles). (Please note that the figure in the digital edition is displayed

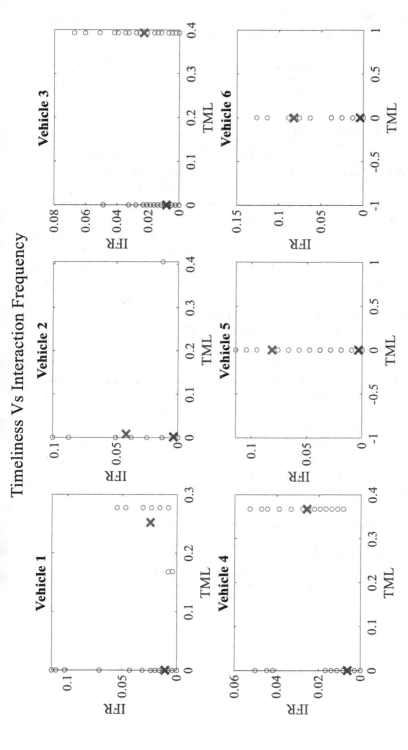

Figure 5.6 Clustering for Labels using Unsupervised Learning for Timeliness vs. Interaction Frequency for vehicles 1 – 6 (The cluster in blue represents *untrustworthy* vehicles whereas the cluster in red depicts *trustworthy* vehicles). (Please note that the figure in the digital edition is displayed with color.)

FM2 into two clusters is depicted in Fig. 5.7. To facilitate visuality, the clustering for each pair of features is depicted. The vehicles belonging to the cluster closer to origin are labeled as malicious, whereas, the members of the cluster farther from the origin are labeled as trustworthy. In Fig. 5.2, vehicles 5 and 6 exhibit no values as both the PDR and TML for all these vehicles are zero, therefore, no clustering can be performed.

5.4.2 CLASSIFICATION MODEL

The overall accuracy, malicious node classification accuracy, precision, recall, F1-score, and decision boundary using each feature matrix for each classifier have been computed for performance evaluation purposes. Simulation results revealed that the classification via mean parametric scores yielded more accurate results, as shown in Fig. 5.16 in contrast to the one which takes into account the parametric score of each trustor for a trustee on an individual basis, as shown in Fig. 5.15. It could be observed that the minimum overall classification accuracy while taking mean parametric score is yielded by Cosine KNN, Cubic KNN and Medium KNN as 94.7%, whereas, while using individual parametric scores, the minimum overall classification accuracy is yielded by Cubic KNN and Subspace Discriminant and is found to be 88.2%. It is also pertinent to highlight that the best malicious vehicle classification result of the proposed trust management model is yielded by taking the mean parametric scores and via Subspace Discriminant.

Figures 5.17 and 5.18 depict the performance evaluation of the envisaged trust model with respect to malicious node classification in terms of precision, recall, and F1-score for individual and mean parametric scores, respectively. Precision is actually defined as the accuracy of the model to classify malicious nodes as malicious, whereas, recall is the proportion of the malicious nodes that have been correctly identified. F1-score represents the weighted mean of the two. All the three performance evaluation metrics mentioned above ranges from *0* to *1*, i.e., *0* represents the worst and *1* represents the best performing model. It can be noted that Subspace KNN yields a perfect precision, recall, and the F1-score equal to 1 for individual parametric scores, whereas Subspace Discriminant returns an ideal precision, recall, and the F1-score equal to 1 for mean parametric scores. Figure 5.8 illustrates the pair-wise decision boundaries between the *trustworthy* and *untrustworthy* vehicles using Subspace KNN classifier for mean parametric scores, whereas, Figs. 5.9– 5.14 demonstrate the pair-wise decision boundaries between the *trustworthy* and *untrustworthy* vehicles using Subspace KNN classifier for individual parametric scores.

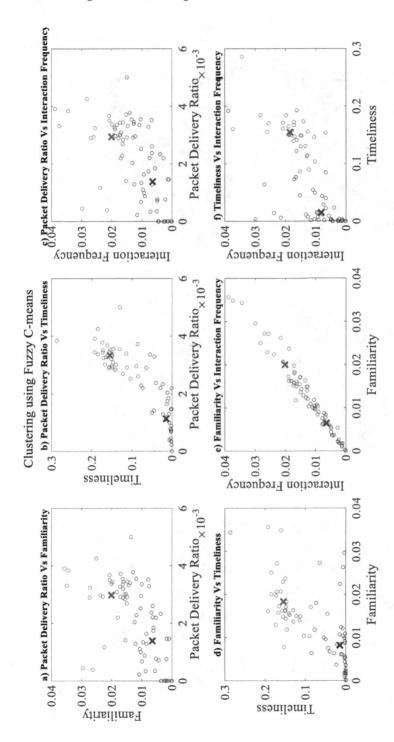

Figure 5.7 Clustering for Labels using Unsupervised Learning a) Packet Delivery Ratio *vs.* Familiarity, b) Packet Delivery Ratio *vs.* Timeliness, c) Packet Delivery Ratio *vs.* Interaction Frequency, d) Familiarity *vs.* Timeliness, e) Familiarity *vs.* Interaction Frequency, and f) Timeliness *vs.* Interaction Frequency (The cluster in blue represents *untrustworthy* vehicles whereas the cluster in red depicts *trustworthy* vehicles). (Please note that the figure in the digital edition is displayed with color.)

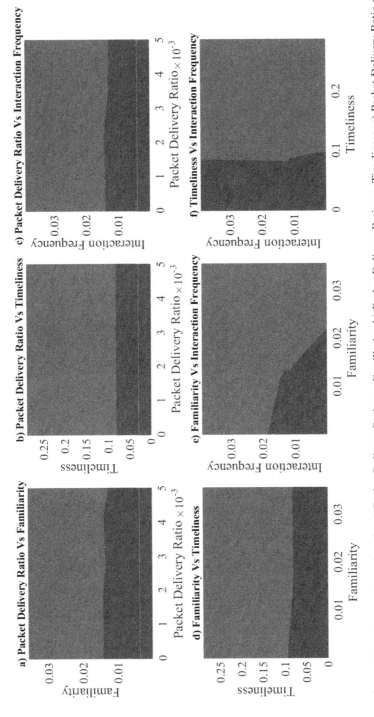

Figure 5.8 Decision Boundary for a) Packet Delivery Ratio vs. Familiarity, b) Packet Delivery Ratio vs. Timeliness, c) Packet Delivery Ratio vs. Interaction Frequency, d) Familiarity vs. Timeliness, e) Familiarity vs. Interaction Frequency, and f) Timeliness vs. Interaction Frequency (Boundary for *untrustworthy* vehicles is depicted in blue, whereas, red manifests the *trustworthy vehicles'* region). (Please note that the figure in the digital edition is displayed with color.)

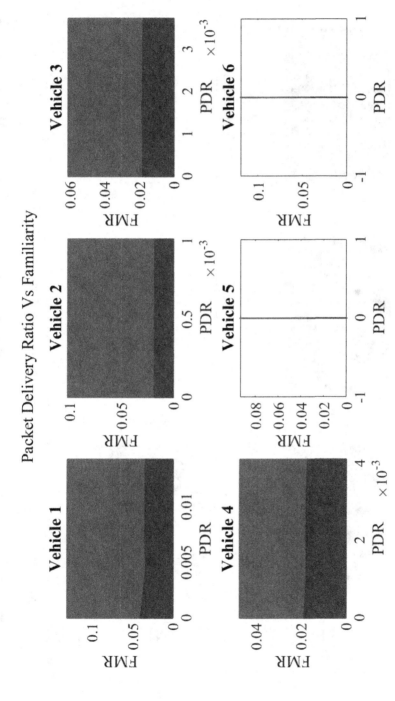

Figure 5.9 Decision Boundary for Packet Delivery Ratio *vs.* Familiarity for vehicles 1 – 6 (Boundary for *untrustworthy* vehicles is depicted in blue, whereas, red manifests the *trustworthy* vehicles' region). (Please note that the figure in the digital edition is displayed with color.)

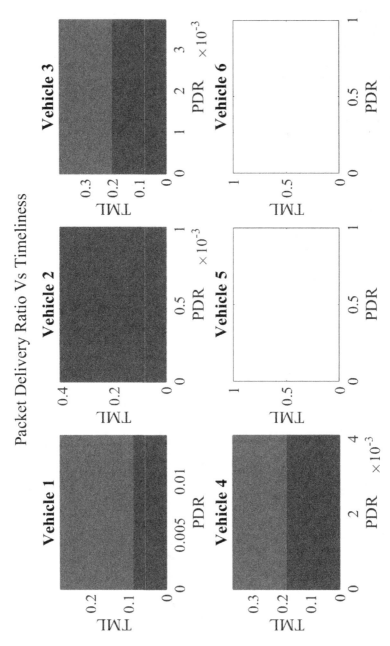

Figure 5.10 Decision Boundary for Packet Delivery Ratio *vs.* Timeliness for vehicles 1 – 6 (Boundary for *untrustworthy* vehicles is depicted in blue, whereas, red manifests the *trustworthy* vehicles' region). (Please note that the figure in the digital edition is displayed with color.)

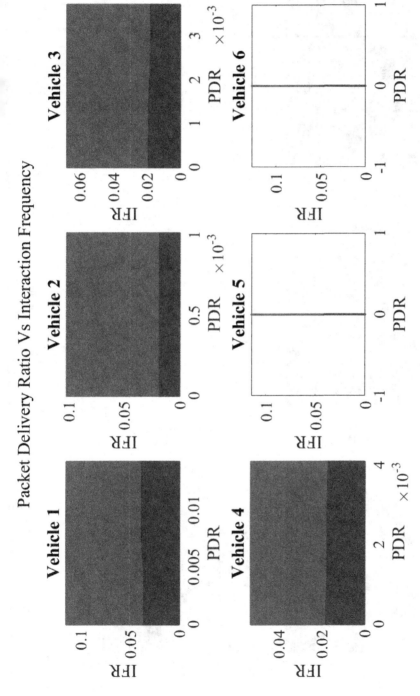

Figure 5.11 Decision Boundary for Packet Delivery Ratio *vs.* Interaction Frequency for vehicles 1 – 6 (Boundary for *untrustworthy* vehicles is depicted in blue, whereas, red manifests the *trustworthy* vehicles' region). (Please note that the figure in the digital edition is displayed with color.)

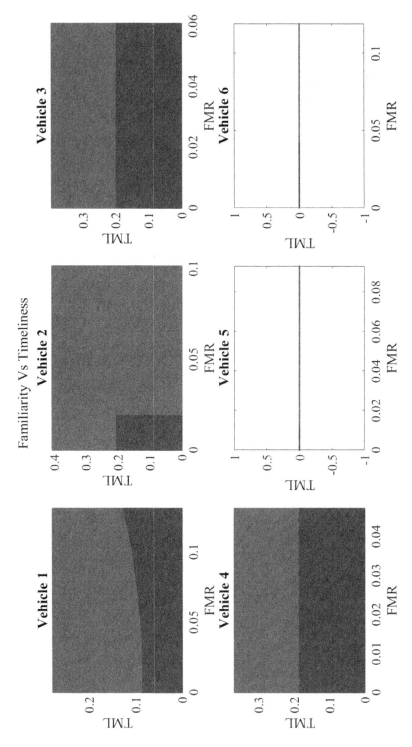

Figure 5.12 Decision Boundary for Familiarity vs. Timeliness for vehicles 1 – 6 (Boundary for *untrustworthy* vehicles is depicted in blue, whereas, red manifests the *trustworthy* vehicles' region). (Please note that the figure in the digital edition is displayed with color.)

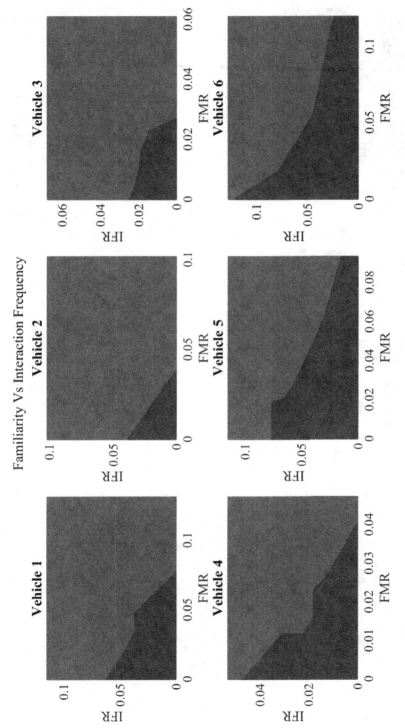

Figure 5.13 Decision Boundary for Familiarity *vs.* Interaction Frequency for vehicles 1 – 6 (Boundary for *untrustworthy* vehicles is depicted in blue, whereas, red manifests the *trustworthy* vehicles' region). (Please note that the figure in the digital edition is displayed with color.)

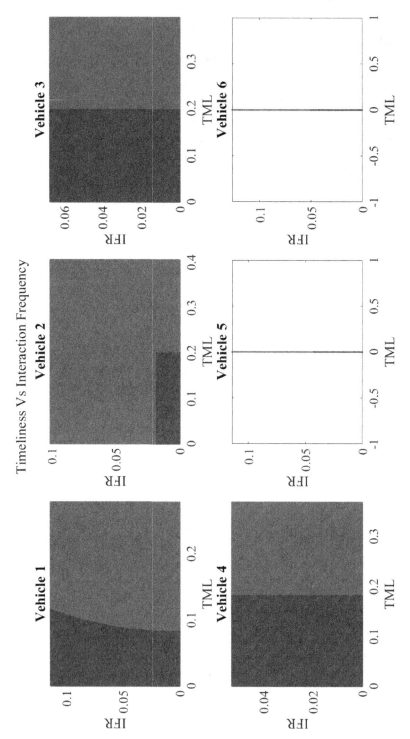

Figure 5.14 Decision Boundary for Timeliness vs. Interaction Frequency for vehicles 1 – 6 (Boundary for *untrustworthy* vehicles is depicted in blue, whereas, red manifests the *trustworthy* vehicles' region). (Please note that the figure in the digital edition is displayed with color.)

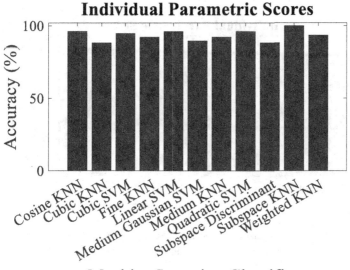

Figure 5.15 Classification Accuracy for Individual Parametric Scores using Different Machine Learning Classifiers. (Please note that the figure in the digital edition is displayed with color.)

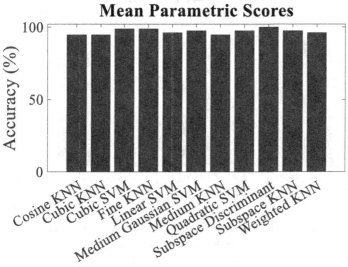

Figure 5.16 Classification Accuracy for Mean Parametric Scores using Different Machine Learning Classifiers. (Please note that the figure in the digital edition is displayed with color.)

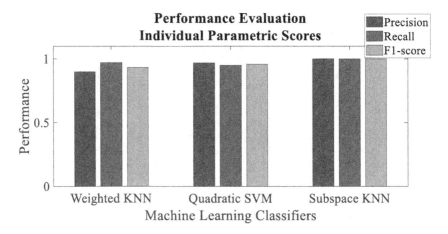

Figure 5.17 Performance Evaluation of Individual Parametric Scores for Malicious Vehicle Classification. (Please note that the figure in the digital edition is displayed with color.)

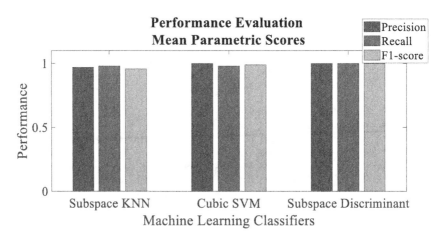

Figure 5.18 Performance Evaluation of Mean Parametric Scores for Malicious Vehicle Classification. (Please note that the figure in the digital edition is displayed with color.)

5.5 CHAPTER SUMMARY

In this chapter, we have proposed a machine learning based distributed trust management model that takes into account the notion of packet delivery ratio, familiarity, timeliness, and interaction frequency amongst the vehicles and employs supervised learning to aggregate/accumulate a vehicle's trust score to identify and subsequently eradicate multiple malicious vehicles in real-time by computing an optimal trust threshold. Simulation results manifest the significance of the selected feature parameters in the classification of dishonest vehicles. Prior to applying supervised learning, two different feature matrices have been generated, one by averaging each parameter for all vehicles and the other with each parameter calculated for each pair of vehicles individually. The classification accuracy for each of the matrices have been evaluated and the decision boundaries are estimated. Simulation results revealed that the classification via the mean parametric scores yielded much more accurate results in contrast to the one which takes into account the parametric score of each trustor for a trustee on an individual basis. It can be noted that Subspace KNN yields a perfect precision, recall, and the F1-score equal to 1 for individual parametric scores, whereas Subspace Discriminant returns an ideal precision, recall, and the F1-score equal to 1 for mean parametric scores.

REFERENCES

1. H. Hasrouny, A. E. Samhat, C. Bassil, and A. Laouiti. *Misbehavior Detection and Efficient Revocation within VANET.* Journal of Information Security and Applications 46, 193 (2019).
2. K. Tan, D. Bremner, J. Le Kernec, L. Zhang, and M. Imran. *Machine Learning in Vehicular Networking: An Overview.* Digital Communications and Networks (2021).
3. H. Ye, L. Liang, G. Y. Li, J. Kim, L. Lu, and M. Wu. *Machine Learning for Vehicular Networks: Recent Advances and Application Examples.* IEEE Vehicular Technology Magazine 13(2), 94 (2018).
4. N. Haddadou, A. Rachedi, and Y. Ghamri-Doudane. *A Job Market Signaling Scheme for Incentive and Trust Management in Vehicular Ad Hoc Networks.* IEEE Transactions on Vehicular Technology 64(8), 3657 (2015).
5. S. Guleng, C. Wu, X. Chen, X. Wang, T. Yoshinaga, and Y. Ji. *Decentralized Trust Evaluation in Vehicular Internet of Things.* IEEE Access 7, 15980 (2019).
6. Z. Lu, Q. Wang, G. Qu, and Z. Liu. *BARS: A Blockchain-based Anonymous Reputation System for Trust Management in VANETs.* In *2018 17th IEEE International Conference on Trust, Security and Privacy in Computing and Communications/12th IEEE International Conference on Big Data Science and Engineering (TrustCom/BigDataSE)*, pp. 98–103 (IEEE, 2018).
7. T. Zhang and Q. Zhu. *Distributed Privacy-preserving Collaborative Intrusion Detection Systems for VANETs.* IEEE Transactions on Signal and Information Processing over Networks 4(1), 148 (2018).
8. M. Aloqaily, S. Otoum, I. Al Ridhawi, and Y. Jararweh. *An Intrusion Detection System for Connected Vehicles in Smart Cities.* Ad Hoc Networks 90, 101842 (2019).

9. E. A. Shams, A. Rizaner, and A. H. Ulusoy. *Trust Aware Support Vector Machine Intrusion Detection and Prevention System in Vehicular Ad Hoc Networks*. Computers Security 78, 245 (2018).

10. J. Grover, N. K. Prajapati, V. Laxmi, and M. S. Gaur. *Machine Learning Approach for Multiple Misbehavior Detection in VANET*. In A. Abraham, J. L. Mauri, J. F. Buford, J. Suzuki, and S. M. Thampi, eds., *Advances in Computing and Communications*, pp. 644–653 (Springer Berlin Heidelberg, Berlin, Heidelberg, 2011).

11. A. K. Jain and R. C. Dubes. *Algorithms for Clustering Data* (Prentice-Hall, Inc., 1988).

12. K. P. Sinaga and M.-S. Yang. *Unsupervised K-means Clustering Algorithm*. IEEE Access 8, 80716 (2020).

13. A. Pugazhenthi and L. S. Kumar. *Selection of Optimal Number of Clusters and Centroids for K-means and Fuzzy C-means Clustering: A Review*. In *2020 5th International Conference on Computing, Communication and Security (ICCCS)*, pp. 1–4 (IEEE, 2020).

14. M.-P. Hosseini, A. Hosseini, and K. Ahi. *A Review on Machine Learning for EEG Signal Processing in Bioengineering*. IEEE Reviews in Biomedical Engineering 14, 204 (2020).

15. A. Pugazhenthi and J. Singhai. *Automatic Centroids Selection in K-means Clustering based Image Segmentation*. In *2014 International Conference on Communication and Signal Processing*, pp. 1279–1284 (IEEE, 2014).

16. B. Yuan, G. J. Klir, and J. F. Swan-Stone. *Evolutionary Fuzzy C-means Clustering Algorithm*. In *Proceedings of 1995 IEEE International Conference on Fuzzy Systems.*, vol. 4, pp. 2221–2226 (IEEE, 1995).

17. A. Pugazhenthi, G. Sreenivasulu, and A. Indhirani. *Background Removal by Modified Fuzzy C-means Clustering Algorithm*. In *2015 IEEE International Conference on Engineering and Technology (ICETECH)*, pp. 1–3 (IEEE, 2015).

18. M. Usama, J. Qadir, A. Raza, H. Arif, K.-L. A. Yau, Y. Elkhatib, A. Hussain, and A. Al-Fuqaha. *Unsupervised Machine Learning for Networking: Techniques, Applications and Research Challenges*. IEEE access 7, 65579 (2019).

19. R. Wang, J. Zhou, X. Liu, S. Han, L. Wang, and Y. Chen. *Transfer Clustering based on Gaussian Mixture Model*. In *2019 IEEE Symposium Series on Computational Intelligence (SSCI)*, pp. 2522–2526 (IEEE, 2019).

20. M.-m. Gao, C. Tai-hua, and X.-x. Gao. *Application of Gaussian Mixture Model Genetic Algorithm in Data Stream Clustering Analysis*. In *2010 IEEE International Conference on Intelligent Computing and Intelligent Systems*, vol. 3, pp. 786–790 (IEEE, 2010).

21. J. Diaz-Rozo, C. Bielza, and P. Larrañaga. *Clustering of Data Streams with Dynamic Gaussian Mixture Models: An IoT Application in Industrial Processes*. IEEE Internet of Things Journal 5(5), 3533 (2018).

22. U. S. Shanthamallu and A. Spanias. *Machine and Deep Learning Algorithms and Applications*. Synthesis Lectures on Signal Processing 12(3), 1 (2021).

23. P. K. Kushwaha and M. Kumaresan. *Machine Learning Algorithm in Healthcare System: A Review*. In *2021 International Conference on Technological Advancements and Innovations (ICTAI)*, pp. 478–481 (IEEE, 2021).

24. G. Chitralekha and J. M. Roogi. *A Quick Review of ML Algorithms*. In *2021 6th International Conference on Communication and Electronics Systems (ICCES)*, pp. 1–5 (IEEE, 2021).

25. B. Verma and A. Rahman. *Cluster-oriented Ensemble Classifier: Impact of Multicluster Characterization on Ensemble Classifier Learning*. IEEE Transactions on Knowledge and Data Engineering 24(4), 605 (2011).

26. S. Rasheed, D. W. Stashuk, and M. S. Kamel. *Integrating Heterogeneous Classifier Ensembles for EMG Signal Decomposition based on Classifier Agreement.* IEEE Transactions on Information Technology in Biomedicine 14(3), 866 (2009).

27. M. Amasyali and O. Ersoy. *Comparison of Single and Ensemble Classifiers in Terms of Accuracy and Execution Time.* In *2011 International Symposium on Innovations in Intelligent Systems and Applications*, pp. 470–474 (IEEE, 2011).

6 Conclusion

6.1 BOOK SUMMARY

The recent evolutionary technological developments in the Internet of Vehicles (IoV) amalgamated with the paradigm of trust have been of considerable interest for experts in the intelligent transportation systems. Smart connected vehicles in an IoV, relying on Vehicle-to-Everything (V2X) communications, aid in providing safe and efficacious traffic flows, subsequently, supporting next-generation road mobility and transport [1]. V2X communications encompass Vehicle-to-Vehicle (V2V), Vehicle-to-Infrastructure (V2I), Vehicle-to-Sensor (V2S), Vehicle-to-Pedestrian (V2P) and Vehicle-to-Cloud (V2C) communications, wherein vehicles utilize wireless media to exchange information with other vehicles, surrounding infrastructure, on-board sensors, personal devices, and the cloud computing environment, respectively [2, 3]. The V2X-based application scenarios generally include i) safety-critical applications, e.g., road congestion, crash avoidance, and collision notification, ii) non-safety applications, e.g., navigation, anti-theft, and iii) entertainment [4].

The recent breakthroughs in Intelligent Transportation Systems (ITS) are primarily related to the acquisition and processing of high volumes of sensor data [5, 6]. The data acquired by the embedded sensors are exchanged with other onboard sensors and with diverse sensors in the vicinity to provide real-time traffic management and ensure road safety [7]. It is, therefore, crucial that the information itself and the exchange of this information are secure and reliable. However, vehicular networks are susceptible to attacks, wherein dishonest entities can modify legitimate safety messages, spread counterfeited information, or forward messages with a delay, subsequently, endangering human lives [8]. The ever-evolving topology owing to the highly mobile nature of vehicular networks, decentralized architecture, pervasive operation, and open infrastructure make it challenging to ensure security and make vehicular networks vulnerable to both insider and outsider attacks [9, 10]. A comprehensive review of the literature demonstrates that numerous cryptography-based security solutions have been suggested, however, these techniques alone have only been proven useful with outsider attacks, wherein the attackers are unauthorized users of the network [11]. To tackle insider attacks on vehicular networks, the notion of trust has lately been introduced and several trust management models have been proposed [12]. Trust is defined as the belief of a vehicle (referred to as a trustor) in its peer vehicle (referred to as a trustee) relying on the past interactions among the two and the opinions towards a trustee, acquired by a trustor's neighboring vehicles.

Trust computation in the said trust management models takes into account numerous parameters, e.g., quality of past interactions (i.e., packet delivery ratio), neighbor recommendations, time, distance, familiarity, frequency of interactions, and amalgamate these parameters to compute the final trust value. While accumulating these parameters, weights are often associated with individual parameters to reflect their

DOI: 10.1201/9781032723662-6

significance in the final trust score. In order to decide which vehicles are honest and which are not, a threshold is defined and vehicles having a trust value above this predefined threshold are categorized as trustworthy. If the trust score of a vehicle falls below the said threshold, that vehicle is identified as a malicious vehicle, and information received only from a trusted vehicle is accepted.

Nevertheless, determining logical and reasonable values for the associated weights is a challenging issue that requires in-depth research. Moreover, deciding a precise value for the misbehavior detection threshold demands considerable attention as setting the value too low or too high may lead to inaccurate categorization of honest and dishonest vehicles. In addition, the consideration of historical behavior along with the introduction of an appropriate time-dependant influence and retribution for dishonest conduct in the past are essential constituents to cater for attack resistance in a trust model. Besides, the introduction of context information is of great significance and could enhance the trust evaluation substantially. Additionally, the time-based analysis of the computed trust concerning the suitability of a particular vehicle for a specific application is of great essence. Furthermore, exploring multiple computational techniques is also crucial to address shortcomings of the existing solutions and open challenges in the domain. Accordingly, the main research contributions of this thesis are summarized as follows.

Literature Review on Trust Management in the Internet of Vehicles: This chapter presented a comprehensive review of the state-of-the-art trust management models in the IoV employing diverse computational domains, e.g., Bayesian inference, blockchain, fuzzy logic, and machine learning. This work emphasized on comparing the said trust management schemes in respect of the simulation tools utilized for performance evaluation, quantification of weights applied while trust aggregation, misbehavior detection incorporated in addition to trust management, attack resistance, and quantification of the threshold defined for misbehavior detection. Furthermore, a brief glimpse of the IoV layered architecture, the notion of trust and its constituents, e.g., similarity, familiarity, timeliness, packet delivery ratio, cooperativeness, and the attacks associated with vehicular networks, e.g., active, passive, malicious, selfish, insider, and outsider attacks, has also been provided. Finally, open challenges in the area have been discussed as well. In a nutshell, this survey can provide useful guidance for future research in trust management in the IoV.

Context-aware Trust Management in the Internet of Vehicles: This chapter focused on developing a trust management scheme relying on diverse influencing parameters, e.g., packet delivery ratio, interaction frequency, timeliness (i.e., time decay), confidence factor, delay, cooperativeness, and familiarity, coupled with the context of the messages exchanged between vehicles. Moreover, it addressed the challenging issues concerning weight quantification by associating rational weights computed via utilizing contributing attributes related to the network and communication dynamics. Furthermore, it catered for resilience against misbehavior, e.g., on-off attacks, and selective node attacks, while formulating constituents of trust and employing a flexible and adaptive threshold to mitigate dishonest vehicles which aligns well with the requirements of the ever-changing vehicular networks. At the beginning, pairwise local trust has been computed which is an amalgamation of the pairwise direct and indirect trusts. The direct trust encompasses the packet delivery ratio as the measure for direct observation, time decay as a weight to incorporate the notion of timeliness, and forgetting factor to penalize for the past misconduct. The indirect trust is a combination of the direct trust of a neighbor as the measure for recommendation or indirect observation and confidence factor as a weight to take account for the credibility of the recommender. The accumulation of the direct and the indirect trusts exploits the frequency of interactions among nodes as a weight to decide the impact of direct and indirect observations on the final trust based on the network dynamics. This pairwise local trust is integrated with the pairwise context-dependant trust that takes into consideration the context of the messages exchanged among vehicles to factor in the sensitivity and criticality of the communication, the distance between the nodes along with the cooperativeness and the familiarity of the nodes. Finally, the pairwise local and context trust are aggregated to evaluate the global trust of each node prior to applying the adaptive misbehavior detection threshold to identify dishonest nodes in the vehicular network. Trust management models can be subjective to the information availability regarding the communication among vehicles and the network dynamics, i.e., datasets. It will be beneficial to use a variety of datasets to envisage trust evaluation frameworks.

Time-aware Trust Management in the Internet of Vehicles: In this chapter, a time-aware trust management model has been proposed utilizing a different dataset (i.e., a real IoT dataset) that addresses the quantification of weights (in the form of timeliness and interaction frequency) associated with the contributing parameters (e.g., familiarity and packet delivery ratio) and the quantification of trust by quantifying the said contributing parameters as well as their weights. Moreover, the impact of weights on each parameter along with the influence of individual parameters on the aggregated trust score has been discussed. Furthermore, our analysis reflected the time-based analysis of the vehicles' trust which facilitates in studying the behavioral patterns of individual vehicles and further investigated the trust-based patterns for safety-critical and non-safety vehicular applications. The pairwise trust among vehicles is computed by taking the weighted sum of packet delivery ratio and familiarity with timeliness, to factor in the freshness of data/interaction between the two nodes, and frequency of interaction, to integrate how often they interact with each other, as weights. Subsequently, this pairwise trust is averaged to calculate the final trust of each trustee. The trust has been evaluated in four different segments with respect to time, i.e., percentage of recent interactions 25, 50, 75, and 100. In addition, a comparison has been presented by employing the proposed weights to associating equal weights with all the contributing parameters prior to discussing and analyzing the application based suitability of individual nodes relying on the computed trust values. The said analysis encompass the study of time-based patterns of two trust evaluation models envisaged in Chapter 3 and 4, respectively.

Machine Learning-based Trust Management in the Internet of Vehicles: In this chapter, we have proposed a distributed trust management model that takes into account the notion of packet delivery ratio, familiarity, timeliness, and interaction frequency amongst the vehicles and employs supervised learning to aggregate/accumulate a vehicle's trust score to identify and subsequently eradicate multiple malicious vehicles in real-time by computing an optimal trust threshold. Simulation results manifested the significance of the selected feature parameters in the classification of dishonest vehicles. Initially, the pairwise contributing parameters of packet delivery ratio, familiarity, timeliness and interaction frequency are computed prior to employing unsupervised learning to assign labels to these calculated values utilizing multiple algorithms, e.g., k-means clustering, fuzzy c-means clustering, hierarchical clustering and Gaussian mixture. These labels are associated in two different ways; by taking each pairwise contributing parameter as a separate feature, and by taking the average of each contributing parameter as a separate feature. Subsequently supervised learning algorithms, e.g., support vector machine, k-nearest neighbors, and ensemble classification algorithms, have been applied to each feature matrix individually to identify dishonest nodes and also to determine the value of the misbehavior detection threshold.

6.2   FUTURE RESEARCH DIRECTIONS

As mentioned in Chapter 2, the cloud layer offers data analyses along with data storage for large volumes of data acquired by vehicles by utilizing on-board sensors and sensors in their immediate vicinity. Recently, Intent-based Networking (IBN) has been introduced in ITS, wherein the notions of Artificial Intelligence (AI) and Machine Learning (ML) have been employed for system management, to analyze this data to provide end-to-end network services [13]. To maximize user experience and to train AI and ML algorithms, the data is collected from vehicles and edge devices continuously. This leads to the edge devices having sufficient information regarding the network and its operations which makes the entire system vulnerable to privacy concerns even if there is a single malicious edge device. It is, therefore, of paramount importance that privacy-preserving techniques are applied on such critical information prior to its reception at the edge device. Developing such techniques for vehicular networks is specially challenging due to the dynamic nature of these networks [14].

6.2.1   PRIVACY AND TRUST MANAGEMENT

The participating IoV entities need to establish trust among one another to sustain a cooperative environment where vehicles are willing to share information as well as use the other services offered by an IoV. The privacy problem augments even further when the notion of trust is applied to vehicular networks. Towards building such confidence on peer entities, several parameters are taken into account, including, but not limited to, the location, distance, communication and network related attributes. The sharing of such sensitive information can lead to an increased susceptibility of these network participants to several attacks. One way to mitigate such privacy issues is to only collect minimal data required, however, this can seriously affect the quality of the services [15].

Another way of preserving privacy is to employ algorithms to maintain the data as well as private information security. For instance, K-anonymity algorithm, which is accurate along with being less compute intensive, has been widely applied for protecting privacy. There are two different designs for these algorithms: 1) centralized, wherein user information is protected utilizing a central server that is trustworthy and anonymous causing performance bottlenecks and a single point of failure, and 2) distributed, wherein the control is divided among several devices which alleviate the above mentioned bottlenecks, however, the participating entities find it difficult to trust one another [16]. This trust dilemma can be resolved by introducing the notion of trust, consequently, both privacy and trust related concerns can be addressed.

Blockchain-based Mechanisms: Due to the highly mobile and dynamic nature of vehicular networks, and performance limitations of the same, centralized trust management architecture is not appropriate and instead, a distributed trust evaluation design would be best suited. Moreover, it is equally important that the said trust model is accumulated to resist any tampering or inconsistencies concerning the stored trust related information. The paradigm of Blockchain has been extensively employed due its distributed structure to support the mobility, dynamicity, and performance requirements of vehicular networks in conjunction with offering data preservation [16, 17]. Owing to the unique characteristics, e.g., distributed structure, trustworthy communication, tamper-resistant records, and entities' anonymity, it also enables edge devices to exchange information while maintaining the database consistency. Even if some edge devices are compromised by attackers, the honest edge devices are still faster in block generation as compared to the dishonest entities [18].

Federated Learning: As indicated previously, AI and ML provide the capability of learning based on the experience and implementing this knowledge to refine models without the need of programming specifically. In vehicular networks, they can prove useful in analyzing vehicle data to study not just about vehicles' activities but also about driving conditions and environment. This involves forwarding large volumes of data acquired by sensors to the centralized server for analysis. Due to a high volume, it gets tricky to store and transmit this data. Moreover, the private details in the said data can pose privacy concerns. Recently, the cutting edge technology of federated learning has attracted the interest of researchers in all domains. The distinguishing feature of this learning technique is that the learning parameters instead of the entire data are sent to the centralized server, whereas, the model training transpires on the vehicle level which decreases the computational overhead of the central server, and mitigates privacy issues in addition to the reduction in data volume to be forwarded [19]. In other words, it offers privacy preserving decentralized learning, where the vehicles acquire the global model prior to initiating the local training/learning process utilizing the same model and their local set of data. Subsequently, the trained model is sent to the central server after employing approaches to protect privacy [20].

Federated Learning (FL) is capable of realizing privacy preservation in addition to data value forwarding, however, the limitations concerning inter-service/domain data sharing, and the trusted application process supervision need to be addressed.

To tackle these shortcomings, blockchain can be implemented combination with federated learning to take advantage of the strengths of both technologies [21, 22].

Reminiscent to other computational techniques, FL is also susceptible to numerous attacks, including, but not limited to, 1) byzantine attacks, wherein the dishonest entities counterfeit legitimate models or parametric updates (i.e., gradients) to undermine the training phase and/or distort the data itself (i.e., the data used for training purposes) to cause incorrect information to be learned by the global model [23, 24], and 2) sybil attacks, wherein a malicious entity enhances the strength and effectiveness of its attack by collaboration, i.e., utilizing sybils, making it more destructive, e.g., sybil relying model poisoning [23, 25, 26]. Such attacks lead to trust issues among the entities in a federated learning environment and one of the open challenges related to FL concerns guaranteeing and establishing trust. The confidence of an FL server towards the testing phase accuracy or other information presented by different entities/users is crucial specially because of the data being held privately on individual devices, manual validation is not an option. In order to ensure secure computation, cryptography-based solutions, e.g., garbled circuits and zero knowledge proofs can be implemented, however, they are impractical for large scale application. MixMatch is a semi-supervised learning technique that does not require precise labels and can be employed for pre-training of computer vision models. Subsequently, accumulation of multiple individual models along with fine-tuning the same utilizing a holdout subset of the dataset are carried out by centralized servers [27].

6.2.2   DATA AVAILABILITY AND TRUST MANAGEMENT

Trust Management Datasets: One of the biggest challenges in devising effective trust management solutions for IoV networks is the unavailability of public datasets in the domain that contain the relative information on the contributing trust attributes in addition to performance evaluation parameters besides ground truths. Building IoV Trust related testbeds can be beneficial in gathering the datasets as well.

Trust Management Testbeds: Several simulation tools, e.g., Veins, SUMO, OMNetpp, and MATLAB, have been employed to realize IoV networks and mobility to evaluate the performance of the proposed trust management schemes. The simulations carried on these tools are comprehensive, however, they are unable to demonstrate the true nature of an IoV network. Moreover, the trust evaluation frameworks utilize a number of trust influencing attributes to compute trust values and evaluate the performance based on a varied set of parameters. Accordingly, a realistic IoV-based testbed is of significant importance for the assessment and comparisons of the envisaged trust management models to provide optimal and efficient solutions. Nevertheless, developing these testbeds is a challenge on its own [28].

Cold Start in Trust Management: Owing to the high mobility, cold start or bootstrapping is a crucial problem in vehicular trust management models. No information is available regarding the previous interactions for newly joining vehicles which makes it impossible to compute the trust score relying on the historical interactions for a newcomer. Consequently, a static initial trust value is assigned to all incoming vehicles. If the said initial value is kept too low, there is a high chance that an honest vehicle will get eliminated from the network owing to a low trust score. On the contrary, if it is set too high, it will take too long to eradicate dishonest nodes (based on trust scores), consequently, jeopardizing the network security. The bootstrapping issue has been addressed in social networks and recommender systems, nevertheless, it is still a major challenge in vehicular trust management models [29].

Data Scarcity in Trust Management: Due to the highly dynamic topology of vehicular networks, scarcity of information availability can lead to ineffective trust management and failure to identify misbehaving entities. Analogous to the cold start problem, data scarcity is caused by minimal or no prior interactions by a vehicle in the network. In the case of a newcomer vehicle, there are no historical interactions, whereas in a low traffic density scenario, there is a limited number of interactions available. Accurate trust computations and vehicle eviction relying on these computations require sufficient information regarding a vehicle's past experiences with its peers. Amalgamating both direct and indirect observations regarding a target vehicle occasionally helps with data scarcity, however, trust management models relying primarily on entity-based trust do not perform well in sparse environments [29].

Threat Models in Trust Management: Misbehavior in vehicular networks can present itself in various forms such as by vehicles acting intelligently, vehicles trying to eavesdrop on others and/or collusion of multiple vehicles. A comprehensive threat or attack model, depicting realistic trust based attack behaviors is of extreme importance. Moreover, in order for the misbehavior detection module to identify a variety of dishonest behaviors and also to punish the dishonest vehicles, the possibility of the participating nodes exhibiting diverse behaviors should be considered. In addition to the detection of misbehavior, robustness of trust management models is of great essence as it enables these trust evaluation schemes to perform effectively even in the presence of malicious entities [28].

In addition to the aforementioned future research directions, time complexity of the algorithms, lack of substantive trust parameters, and utilization of diverse simulation tools for the implementation of trust management models need to be discussed and investigated.

REFERENCES

1. Y. Xing, C. Lv, and D. Cao. *Personalized Vehicle Trajectory Prediction based on Joint Time-Series Modeling for Connected Vehicles.* IEEE Transactions on Vehicular Technology 69(2), 1341 (2020).
2. M. Hasan, S. Mohan, T. Shimizu, and H. Lu. *Securing Vehicle-to-Everything (V2X) Communication Platforms.* IEEE Transactions on Intelligent Vehicles 5(4), 693 (2020).
3. M. Sepulcre and J. Gozalvez. *Heterogeneous V2V Communications in Multi-Link and Multi-RAT Vehicular Networks.* IEEE Transactions on Mobile Computing 20(1), 162 (2021).
4. M. Hasan, S. Mohan, T. Shimizu, and H. Lu. *Securing Vehicle-to-Everything (V2X) Communication platforms.* IEEE Transactions on Intelligent Vehicles 5(4), 693 (2020).
5. P. Arthurs, L. Gillam, P. Krause, N. Wang, K. Halder, and A. Mouzakitis. *A Taxonomy and Survey of Edge, Cloud Computing for Intelligent Transportation Systems and Connected Vehicles.* IEEE Transactions on Intelligent Transportation Systems (2021).

6. F. Jameel, M. A. Javed, S. Zeadally, and R. Jäntti. *Secure Transmission in Cellular V2X Communications using Deep Q-Learning.* IEEE Transactions on Intelligent Transportation Systems (2022).

7. F. Zhu, Y. Lv, Y. Chen, X. Wang, G. Xiong, and F.-Y. Wang. *Parallel Transportation Systems: Toward IoT-enabled Smart Urban Traffic Control and Management.* IEEE Transactions on Intelligent Transportation Systems 21(10), 4063 (2019).

8. Z. A. Biron, S. Dey, and P. Pisu. *Real-time Detection and Estimation of Denial of Service Attack in Connected Vehicle Systems.* IEEE Transactions on Intelligent Transportation Systems 19(12), 3893 (2018).

9. S. Tangade, S. S. Manvi, and P. Lorenz. *Trust Management Scheme based on Hybrid Cryptography for Secure Communications in VANETs.* IEEE Transactions on Vehicular Technology 69(5), 5232 (2020).

10. M. N. Mejri, J. Ben-Othman, and M. Hamdi. *Survey on VANET Security Challenges and Possible Cryptographic Solutions.* Vehicular Communications 1(2), 53 (2014).

11. S. Tangade, S. S. Manvi, and P. Lorenz. *Decentralized and Scalable Privacy-preserving Authentication Scheme in VANETs.* IEEE Transactions on Vehicular Technology 67(9), 8647 (2018).

12. W. Li and H. Song. *ART: An Attack-Resistant Trust Management Scheme for Securing Vehicular Ad Hoc Networks.* IEEE Transactions on Intelligent Transportation Systems 17(4), 960 (2016).

13. S. Garg, K. Kaur, G. Kaddoum, S. H. Ahmed, and D. N. K. Jayakody. *SDN-based Secure and Privacy-preserving Scheme for Vehicular Networks: A 5G Perspective.* IEEE Transactions on Vehicular Technology 68(9), 8421 (2019).

14. S. Ghane, A. Jolfaei, L. Kulik, K. Ramamohanarao, and D. Puthal. *Preserving Privacy in the Internet of Connected Vehicles.* IEEE Transactions on Intelligent Transportation Systems 22(8), 5018 (2020).

15. E. Zavvos, E. H. Gerding, V. Yazdanpanah, C. Maple, S. Stein, et al. *Privacy and Trust in the Internet of Vehicles.* IEEE Transactions on Intelligent Transportation Systems (2021).

16. B. Li, R. Liang, D. Zhu, W. Chen, and Q. Lin. *Blockchain-based Trust Management Model for Location Privacy Preserving in VANET.* IEEE Transactions on Intelligent Transportation Systems 22(6), 3765 (2020).

17. Y. Zhao, Y. Wang, P. Wang, and H. Yu. *PBTM: A Privacy-preserving Announcement Protocol With Blockchain-based Trust Management for IoV.* IEEE Systems Journal (2021).

18. X. Liu, H. Huang, F. Xiao, and Z. Ma. *A Blockchain-based Trust Management with Conditional Privacy-preserving Announcement Scheme for VANETs.* IEEE Internet of Things Journal 7(5), 4101 (2019).

19. M. Asad, A. Moustafa, and T. Ito. *Federated Learning Versus Classical Machine Learning: A Convergence Comparison.* arXiv preprint arXiv:2107.10976 (2021).

20. M. H. ur Rehman, A. M. Dirir, K. Salah, E. Damiani, and D. Svetinovic. *TrustFed: A Framework for Fair and Trustworthy Cross-device Federated Learning in IoT.* IEEE Transactions on Industrial Informatics 17(12), 8485 (2021).

21. Z. Zhu, J. Hong, and J. Zhou. *Data-free Knowledge Distillation for Heterogeneous Federated Learning.* In *International Conference on Machine Learning*, pp. 12878–12889 (PMLR, 2021).

22. G. Hua, L. Zhu, J. Wu, C. Shen, L. Zhou, and Q. Lin. *Blockchain-based Federated Learning for Intelligent Control in Heavy Haul Railway.* IEEE Access 8, 176830 (2020).

23. N. Rodríguez-Barroso, D. J. López, M. Luzón, F. Herrera, and E. Martínez-Cámara. *Survey on Federated Learning Threats: Concepts, Taxonomy on Attacks and Defences, Experimental Study and Challenges.* arXiv preprint arXiv:2201.08135 (2022).

24. S. Hu, J. Lu, W. Wan, and L. Y. Zhang. *Challenges and Approaches for Mitigating Byzantine Attacks in Federated Learning.* arXiv preprint arXiv:2112.14468 (2021).

25. C. Fung, C. J. Yoon, and I. Beschastnikh. *Mitigating Sybils in Federated Learning Poisoning.* arXiv preprint arXiv:1808.04866 (2018).

26. V. Mothukuri, R. M. Parizi, S. Pouriyeh, A. Dehghantanha, and K.-K. R. Choo. *FabricFL: Blockchain-in-the-Loop Federated Learning for Trusted Decentralized Systems.* IEEE Systems Journal (2021).

27. M. S. Jere, T. Farnan, and F. Koushanfar. *A Taxonomy of Attacks on Federated Learning.* IEEE Security & Privacy 19(2), 20 (2020).

28. A. Mahmood, Q. Z. Sheng, S. A. Siddiqui, S. Sagar, W. E. Zhang, H. Suzuki, and W. Ni. *When Trust Meets the Internet of Vehicles: Opportunities, Challenges, and Future Prospects.* In *2021 IEEE 7th International Conference on Collaboration and Internet Computing (CIC)*, pp. 60–67 (IEEE, 2021).

29. S. A. Siddiqui, A. Mahmood, Q. Z. Sheng, H. Suzuki, and W. Ni. *A Survey of Trust Management in the Internet of Vehicles.* Electronics 10(18), 2223 (2021).

Index

Note: Page numbers in **bold** and *italics* refer to tables and figures, respectively.

A

Active attacks, 17
ADMM (alternating direction method of multipliers) algorithm, 97
Aggregated trust, *61*, **62**
 BTCMV, *63*, **64**
Anomaly-based detection, 97
Artificial intelligence, 94
Attacks, categories of, 17
 active attacks, 17
 insider attacks, 17–18
 malicious attacks, 17
 outsider attacks, 18
 passive attacks, 17
 selfish attacks, 17
Authentication, 3, 29, 69
 framework, 29
 phase, 17

B

Bad-mouthing and ballot stuffing attack, 18
Bayesian inference, 10, 71, 95
 -based decentralized trust model, 23
 -based reputation, 29
 -based trust model, 22–23
Belief function, 23
Big data, 1
Bit torrent, 40
Black-hole attack, 18–19
Blockchain, 10
 based decentralized trust management model, 25
 -based mechanisms, 128
 -based trust model, 24–25, 96
Byzantine attacks, 129

C

Car-Torrent, 40
Certificate blockchain (CertBC), 24
Certification authority (CA), 24–25
CF, *see* Confidence factor
Cloud computing, 1
Cloud layer, 13
CO_2 emissions, 40
Collusion
 attack, 22
 avoidance warning, 39
 warning, 5
Common attacks, 18
 bad-mouthing and ballot stuffing attack, 18
 black-hole attack, 18–19
 man-in-the-middle attack, 18
 on–off attack, 18
 selective behavior attack, 18
 Sybil attack, 18
Confidence factor (CF), 48–49, 85
Confidentiality, 3
Context-aware security, 41
Context-aware trust management, 39
 in IoV, 125–126
 non-safety applications, 40
 safety-critical applications, 39–40
 simulation setup and results, 54–65
 trust management and context-awareness, 40–42
Context-dependant trust, 51–52
 cooperativeness, 51
 familiarity, 51–52
 propagation delay, 51
Context dependent trust trend, **85**
Convex (CVX) tool based on MATLAB, 25

Cooperativeness, 15, 51–52
Co-work relationship, 15
CRAWDAD, 75
    dataset, 95
Cryptography
    -based security solutions, 41
    -based trust model, 28–30
    techniques, 3

D
Data-centric trust management models,
    16
Data dissemination, 16
Data-driven techniques, 94
Data scarcity in trust management, 130
Data source layer, 12–13
Data transmission, 22
Data trust, 19
Deep learning, 25–27
Deep/machine learning-based trust
    model, 25–27
Dempster–Shafer theory, 26
Denial of service attack, 24
Direct trust, 14, *15,* 44–48, 54, *55*
    comparison of results, **65**
    computation, 49
    trend over time, **84**
Dishonest vehicles, 19
Duration of interactions, 15–16

E
Edge computing, 1
Edge layer, 13
Emergency brake notification, 5, 39
Ensemble subspace KNN, 95
Entity-centric trust management models,
    16

F
F1-score, 110
Familiarity, 15, 51–52, 72–73, **80,** 94, 99
Federated learning, 128–129
File sharing services, 40
Fleenet, 40

Fog layer, 13
Forgetting factor, 47–48
    trend, **87**
Frequency of interactions, 16, 50
Fuzzy c-means, 101–102
Fuzzy logic, 10
    based trust models, 27–28
Fuzzy system, 27

G
Gaussian mixture, 101
Global trust, 53, *60*
    trend, **84**
    with/without forgetting factor, *57*
GNU MultiPrecision (GMP), 29

H
Hierarchical clustering, 101
Hybrid trust management models, 17, 21

I
IDS, *see* Intrusion detection system
Indirect trust, 14, *15,* 48–51
    computation, 50
    trend over time, **85**
Infrastructure-to-vehicle trust, 19
Insider attacks, 17–18, 69
Integrity, 3
Intelligent parking navigation systems,
    40
Intelligent transportation systems (ITS),
    1, 94, 124
Interaction frequency, 74, 94, 99
Internet of Things (IoT), 1
Internet of Vehicles (IoV), 1, *2,* 3, 12,
    124
    architecture, 10
    attacks in, *20*
    cloud layer, 13
    data source layer, 12–13
    edge layer, 13
    fog layer, 13
    layered architecture of, *12*
    network, 10, 12

state-of-the-art trust management, 19
   bayesian inference-based trust model, 22–23
   blockchain-based trust model, 24–25
   cryptography-based trust model, 28–30
   deep/machine learning-based trust model, 25–27
   fuzzy logic-based trust models, 27–28
   trust models, 19–22
   trust management in, 3–4
Internet services, 40
Intrusion detection system (IDS), 97
IoV, *see* Internet of Vehicles
IoV-based simulator, 54
ITS, *see* Intelligent transportation systems

J
Joint spectrum sensing, 22
JSSDT, 22

K
K-nearest neighbors (KNN) algorithm, 95, 96, 101, 102

L
LAN, 13
Local trust, 44–51
   computation, 50
   direct trust, 44–48
   indirect trust, 48–51
Location proximity, 16

M
Machine learning, 10, 94, 127
Machine learning based trust management, 94–97
   in IoV, 126–127
   simulation results, 103
     classification model, 110–120
     clustering & labeling, 103–110
   system model, 97–98
     classification model, 102–103
     clustering & labeling, 100–102
     dataset & feature extraction, 99–100
Machine learning techniques, 95
Malicious attacks, 17
Man-in-the-middle attack, 18
MARINE, 19
MATLAB, 21, 23, 25, 26, 27, 28, 54
Message blockchain (MesBC), 24
Misbehavior detection, 53–54
Misbehavior detection scheme, 26
MiXiM, 29
Mobile ad hoc networks (MANETs), 1
MoSim, 28
MOVE, 30

N
Neighbor trust trend, **89**
Networking infrastructure, 13
Network Simulator (NS-3), 26
Newcomer attack, 22
Next-generation road mobility and transport, 2
Node trust, 19
Non-safety applications, 40
Non-safety (infotainment) applications, *41*
Notion of trust, 13–14
NS-3, 30

O
OMNET++ (Objective Modular Network Testbed in C++), 24, 27, 29
On–off attack, 18, 22
OPNET, 26
Outsider attacks, 18

P
Packet delivery ratio (PDR), 15, 44, 54, *55,* 73–74, **80, 86,** 94, 99

Passive attacks, 17
Peer to peer (P2P) applications, 40
Physical unclonable functions (PUF), 24
PKI, *see* Public key infrastructure
Propagation delay, 51–52
Public key infrastructure (PKI), 29

Q
Q-learning, 27

R
Real-time traffic management, 124
Reputation model simulator
(TRMSim-V2V), 28
Revocation blockchain (RevBC),
24
Right/left turn assistance, 40
Road accidents, 1
Roadside unit (RSU), 19, 24, 43, 69
Route navigation, 70

S
Safety-critical vehicular applications,
39–40, *41,* 80
Safety-related information, 55
SDN (software-defined network)
controller, 26
Security solutions, 3
Selective behavior attack, 18
Selfish attacks, 17
Set of vehicles, 44
Similarity, 14–15
Simulation
setup and results, 54–65
of urban mobility (SUMO),
19, 24
Simulator for IoV Dataset, *55*
State-of-the-art trust management,
19
Bayesian inference-based trust
model, 22–23
blockchain-based trust model,
24–25

cryptography-based trust model,
28–30
deep/machine learning-based trust
model, 25–27
fuzzy logic-based trust models,
27–28
trust models, 19–22
Steady threshold vis-'a-vis proposed
adaptive threshold, *66*
SUMO, 27, 29, 30
Support vector machine (SVM), 95, 96,
102
Sybil attack, 18
System architecture, *45*
System framework, *46*
System model
familiarity, 72–73
interaction frequency, 74
packet delivery ratio, 73–74
timeliness, 74

T
Temporal function of truth value, 22
TensorFlow, 26
Time-aware trust management, 69–72
in IoV, 126
simulation setup and results, 75–89
system model, 72–75
Time-based analysis, 70
Time-based models, 70
Time decay, 44, 54
Timeliness, 15, 74, 94, 99
Time proximity, 16
Time series, 70
Time-series data analysis, 70
Time-varying analysis, 5
Total local trust, 52–53
Traffic congestion, 1
warning, 5
Traffic control authority (CCO), 29
Traffic management systems, 1
Trust
assessment, 97
attributes, 14

cooperativeness, 15
co-work relationship, 15
duration of interactions, 15–16
familiarity, 15
frequency of interactions, 16
packet delivery ratio, 15
similarity, 14–15
timeliness, 15
components of, 14
direct trust, 14
indirect trust, 14
computation, 10, 77, 124
defined, 40, 124
evaluation, 95
overview, 14
time-based patterns, 72
time-varying patterns for,
79, 82
trend over time, **78**
Trust authorities and vehicles, 19
Trust-based decision making, 69
Trust-based vehicular security, 4, 5
Trust blockchain (TrustBC), 24
Trustee, 69
Trust evaluation and management for
IoV, 43–44
context-dependant trust, 51–52
global trust, 53
local trust, 44–51
misbehavior detection, 53–54
total local trust, 52–53
Trust for safety-critical communication,
58–59
Trust management, 4, 10, 125
cold start, 129–130
and context-awareness, 40–42
data scarcity in, 130
datasets, 129
in IoV, 125
models, 5, 10, 29, 70, 96
data-centric trust management
models, 16
entity-centric trust management
models, 16

hybrid trust management
models, 17
research challenges, 30
cold start, 30
data scarcity, 31
steady threshold, 31
threshold quantification, 31
weights quantification,
31–32
scheme, 42
testbeds, 129
trust model in, 130
Trust models, 19–22
Trustor, 69, 124
TrustRank algorithm, 22, 72
Trust Value, 5
Trustworthy vehicles, 96

U
Untrustworthy vehicles, 22, 96

V
V2I communications, 13
VANET, 26, 42, 71
VANETMobiSim, 21
VANETS, 22
VANETsim, 29
Vehicles in network simulation
(VEINS), 19
Vehicles sharing information,
65
Vehicle-to-cloud (V2C) communication,
2, 124
Vehicle-to-everything (V2X)
communications, 1–2, 2, 65,
124
Vehicle-to-infrastructure (V2I)
communication, 2, 124
Vehicle-to-pedestrian (V2P)
communication, 2, 124
Vehicle-to-sensor (V2S)
communication, 2, 124
Vehicle-to-vehicle (V2V)
communication, 2, 124

Vehicle-to-vehicle trust, 19
Vehicular ad hoc networks
    (VANETs), 1
Vehicular networks, 3, 94
Vehicular social networks, 21

Vehicular trust management, 22
VEINS, 22, 24, 27, 29

W
Wi-Fi, 13

Printed in the United States
by Baker & Taylor Publisher Services